SHEET PAN COOKBOOK

101-RECIPE BOOK

WITH DELICIOUSLY SIMPLE & HEALTHY SATISFYING HANDS-OFF MEALS STRAIGHT FROM THE OVEN

THOMAS O'NEAL

Leave a review about our book:

As an independent author with a small marketing budget, reviews are my livelihood on this platform. If you enjoyed this book, I'd really appreciate it, if you left your honest feedback. You can do so by clicking review button.

I love hearing my readers and I personally read every single review!

TABLE OF CONTENTS

INTRODUCTION

Sheet pan cooking is by far the most convenient technique to cook large batches of food at a time in the oven. Whether you are roasting vegetables, meat, seafood, or baking cookies or cakes, sheet pans offer a large cooking surface area to provide heat to every bit of food evenly. Sheet pans can be used to cook a variety of meals using different seasonings and flavors. Now you can cook all sorts of the meal using sheet pans at home as we bring you the best of sheet pan recipes in this cookbook. There are recipes for breakfast, making snacks, lunch, dinner, desserts, etc. All you need to do is get the right sheet pan for the right time and let's get started!

CHAPTER 1:

SHEET PAN BASICS

A sheet pan is termed the most versatile pan in the kitchen. They are suitable to adjust meals in a variety of serving sizes. You can pick and choose a sheet pan and bake or roast a variety of dishes.

Why sheet pan?

A sheet pan is just a baking pan, but it is less deep and flatter than regular baking pans. These pans provide greater baking surface area, but unlike baking sheets, they tend to keep the food inside their raised rim boundaries. Sheet pans are particularly popular in restaurants where the food is cooked in large batches, or they are commonly used in home ovens to cook food in a large amount.

You can roast vegetables, bake nachos, toast bread slices, cook bacon, or roast all sorts of steaks, poultry, other beef cuts, seafood, or a combination of these ingredients in a single sheet pan.

Sheet pans provide ease of cooking a variety of things in a single place. You can make rows of items in a sheet pan then roast them together. With the large surface areas, heat is provided to every bit of food.

Why can it be Easy and Healthy?

Sheet pans are the most versatile pans you can have. They are great at roasting vegetables and for cheese melting on nachos. You can make crispy fries or bacon in a sheet pan or use one to broil and cook braised beef, lamb, or pork! You can cook an entire lunch or dinner having meat and vegetables.

Cooking in sheet pans is easy because you get to cook everything in a single place. Plus, it is healthy to cook in sheet pans because all the juices and cooking liquids are preserved in the pan during cooking.

How to Select a Suitable Sheet Pan?

Sheet pans are available in a wide variety and if you want to collect the right type of sheet pans to cook different types of meals, then here is how you can select them:

Size

The sheet pans are available in different sizes; in some countries, the 8x13-inch size is taken as a standard, and it is a good size when you are baking at home for families and friends, but when it comes to professional or commercial baking, the 18x26-inch size is considered the standard. However, there are plenty of other sheet pan sizes that can serve the purpose, and the following is the list of all such sheet pans:

1. Eighth-size sheet pan: The pans are the smallest of all; they are perfect for serving 2–4 people in a single session. Their dimensions are 6 ½ inches x 9 ½ inches x 1 inch.
2. Quarter-size sheet pan: Next in line are these quarter-size sheet pans, which are fit for small or medium-sized servings as their dimensions are 9 ½ inches x 13 inches x 1 inch.
3. Half-sized sheet pan: These rectangular flat sheet pans are also 1-inch deep, but they give you a standard sheet pancake due to its dimensions of 13 inches x 8 inches x 1 inch. This size in sheet pans

is a must-have for every baker because it can serve a variety of purposes.

4. Three-quarter-size sheet pan: Let's just say that you want to bake a cake for a gathering of 10, and you want a pan bigger than the standard but not too big like the full sheet pan, then this size is perfect for you. It has dimensions of 15 inches x 21 inches x 1 inch.

5. Full-sized sheet pan: In the US, 18 inches x 26 inches x 1 inch is considered the standard sheet pan size, and other sizes are compared with it. They are fit to serve an extra-large gathering, and these cake pans are mostly used in bakeries and restaurants to bake slab cakes.

If you want to try all sorts of sheet cakes, then it is best that you buy a complete set of these sheet pans, with each having a different size. This might cost you some extra money, but it will save you time from going and buying a new pan every time you try a different recipe.

Material

When you think of the best heat conduction, what comes to mind is bare aluminum. Yes! It heats up so quickly and then cools down even faster, which means that cakes will start cooking as soon as the pan goes into the oven and stops cooking as soon as it comes out. The aluminum pans are lighter in color, which lets you see clearly the brown color around the edges and the bottoms of the cakes. Aluminized steel is another good material in sheet pans, in which steel is sandwiched in two layers of aluminum, but it can give uneven heat due to differences in the material. Stainless steel is also an available material in these pans, but it is also known for its poor performance.

Nonstick Coating

Nonstick coatings can cause more trouble than good because if you buy a pan with a substandard nonstick coating, then the chances are that it will wear out quickly. Pans with nonstick coating tend to have a darker color, so they absorb more heat and radiate more, which quickly browns your cakes. So, if you are going to get a nonstick sheet pan, make sure to get one with a lasting coating and bake the cakes in this pan with caution to avoid over-browning.

Rolled Edges

Pans with rolled edges are superior to the flat rims of the pan. These pans allow easy covering and handling of the sheet pans. These edges also give these pans a nice finish and smooth look.

Cookie Sheet vs. Sheet Pan

Cookie sheets or baking sheets are entirely different from a sheet pan; they don't have any edges or walls to keep the food inside. You can only cook cookies or items that do not flow in the cookie or baking sheets. At the same time, sheet pans are rimmed pans with ½-inch to 1-inch-high walls to keep the juices, cooking liquid, or other flowing items inside the pan. Alternatively, if you roast the food on the cookie sheet, the juices will run off, and they will create a mess inside the oven. In this way, sheet pans are more suitable to roast meat and vegetables, etc.

Pale vs. dark sheet pan

Dark pans tend to absorb more heat, whereas light baking pans reflect heat, and a difference in this absorption capacity can make all the difference during cooking since dark pans absorb more heat, so they cook the food faster, and they can even burn baked goods. However, that's not the case with the light sheet pans; these pans are more suitable for slow baking like baking cakes, cookies and bread, etc.

If you are using dark pans, then make sure to reduce the heat and the cooking time by 25 percent than the original time to prevent food from overcooking or burning. Place this dark pan on the middle rack and keep checking the food frequently. Once you get to know the differences between the two dark or light types of sheet pans and how they work, you can make adjustments in every recipe accordingly.

Choosing the right lining

It is important to select the right lining to cook food without burning or sticking. There are different things that you can use to line the sheet pans:

- Baking or parchment paper
- Foil sheet
- Butter or cooking spray

Baking paper is the most used liner, which is good at preventing the food from sticking. You can cut it in the desired size. Foil sheets are another good option, and they heat up quickly.

Tips for cooking with sheet pans

1. If you are cooking different types of food like chicken, shrimp, corn cobs, tomatoes, zucchini, etc., in a single session, then add these ingredients to the sheet pan according to their cooking time.
2. Always grease or line the sheet pan from baking paper to prevent uneven cooking or sticking of the food.
3. If you are adding fried food to the sheet, then make sure to spray it with cooking oil.

4. Adjust the cooking temperature according to keeping the large surface area of the sheet pan.
5. Do not fill the sheet pan more than 2/3 of its height with liquid or any batter because the food may overflow out of the sheet pan.

Tips for caring for sheet pans

Most sheet pans that we use today are nonstick, easily washable, and have this coating that keeps them from rusting. However, rough use and lack of care can destroy the condition of your sheet pans. Here is what you should keep in mind while dealing with the sheet pans:

1. Do not scrub the sheet pans with hard scrubbers. If the food is stuck on the surface, make sure to soak the sheet pan in water to soften the food, in particular, then wash with soap water and a sponge.
2. Keep the sheet pan in a dry place in the kitchen. Keep them away from water or other liquids.
3. Always grease the sheet pans before using them.

The Most Important Rules of Sheet Pan Cooking

- Add Food in Stages

If you are cooking different types of food like chicken, shrimp, corn cobs, tomatoes, zucchini, etc., in a single session, then add these ingredients to the sheet pan according to their cooking time.

- Eating Healthy Should Still Be Delicious.

If you are cooking food in sheet pans, make sure to add the necessary seasonings and flavorings to the basic ingredients to infuse the flavors during the cooking process.

- Position Everything Wisely

Set everything in the sheet pan according to its size or cooking time. For instance, if you are cooking whole chicken with potatoes or zucchini, then place the chicken at the center of the sheet and the veggies around it.

- Go for Uniform Sizes

Try to use uniform-sized cuts and pieces for cooking in the sheet pans. In this way, everything will be cooked at the same time. Otherwise, some of the pieces of food will turn out to be undercooked, and others might come out as overcooked.

- Don't Overcrowd the Ingredients

The whole purpose of using the sheet pan is to cook the food in a single layer. If you overcrowd the sheet pan, you will not get the desired results. Make sure to avoid overcrowding.

Table: Vegetable Roasting Times

Vegetable	Temp. ºF	Roasting time
Asparagus	425ºF	15–20 minutes
Green beans	425ºF	15–20 minutes
Okra	425ºF	15 minutes
Crucifers	425ºF	about 20 minutes
Brussels sprouts	375–400ºF	15–20 minutes
Broccoli	350ºF	25 minutes
Cauliflower	400ºF	20–30 minutes
Cabbage, wedges	425ºF	30–40 minutes
Fennel	425ºF	20–30 minutes
Root vegetables, cubed	350–425ºF	20–35 minutes
Sweet potato sticks	425ºF	20–25 minutes
Potato, diced	400ºF	25–30 minutes
Jacket potatoes	350ºF	45 minutes
New potatoes	400ºF	30–40 minutes
Beets, whole (in foil)	350ºF	about 60 minutes
Carrots, cubed or cut into sticks	425ºF	20–30 minutes
Butternut squash, cubed	400ºF	20–25 minutes
Butternut squash, halved	400ºF	40–60 minutes
Acorn squash, halved	450ºF	50–60 minutes
Spaghetti squash, halved	400ºF	30–40 minutes
Summer squash	400–425ºF	15 minutes
Zucchini, cubed	400–425ºF	15 minutes
Breadfruit, halved (ulu)	400ºF	60–80 minutes
Eggplant, cubed	375–400ºF	20–30 minutes
Eggplant, whole or halved	350ºF	45–60 minutes
Bell pepper, cubed	400ºF	15 minutes

Tomatillos	425°F	20 minutes
Tomatoes, cherry or grape	400°F	15–20 minutes
Tomatoes, whole	400°F	40–50 minutes
Corn on the cob	425°F	about 30 minutes
Corn kernels	400°F	15 minutes
Mushrooms	425°F	20–25 minutes
Artichokes, baby	425°F	20–30 minutes
Garlic, whole head	400°F	40 minutes
Garlic, thin slices	400°F	10–15 minutes
Onions, rings	425°F	15–20 minutes
Onions, halved	425°F	30–45 minutes
Vegetable kabobs (veggie skewers)	400°F	15–20 minutes

CHAPTER 2:

BREAKFAST
RECIPES

Coconut Granola

Preparation time: 10 minutes

Cooking time: 18 minutes

Total time: 28 minutes

Servings: 4

Nutritional Values

Calories 200, Total Fat 19.3 g, Saturated Fat 17.2 g, Cholesterol 0 mg,

Sodium 68 mg, Total Carbs 7.3 g, Fiber 4.3 g, Sugar 2.7 g, Protein 1.6 g

Ingredients

- 1 tablespoon coconut oil, melted
- 1 tablespoon coconut butter, melted
- 1 teaspoon orange zest, grated freshly
- ½ teaspoon ground cinnamon
- Pinch of sea salt
- 2 cups coconut flakes

How to Prepare

1. Preheat your oven to 350°F.
2. Line a baking sheet with parchment paper.
3. In a bowl, add coconut oil, coconut butter, orange zest, cinnamon and salt and mix well.
4. Place the coconut flakes onto the prepared baking sheet and spread in an even layer.
5. Pour coconut oil mixture over flakes and gently stir to mix.
6. Bake for approximately 12–15 minutes.
7. Remove the baking sheet of granola from oven and set aside to cool completely before serving.
8. Break the granola into desired-sized chunks and serve with your favorite non-dairy milk.
9. You can preserve this granola in an airtight container.

QUINOA & NUTS GRANOLA

Preparation time: 15 minutes

Cooking time: 15 minutes

Total time: 30 minutes

Servings: 6

Nutritional Values

Calories 281, Total Fat 14.3 g, Saturated Fat 6.7 g, Cholesterol 0 mg,

Sodium 32 mg, Total Carbs 35.3 g, Fiber 4.6 g, Sugar 16.6 g,

Protein 6.5 g

Ingredients

- ¾ cup uncooked red quinoa
- ½ cup coconut flakes
- ½ cup almonds, chopped
- 2 tablespoons chia seeds
- 2 tablespoons pumpkin seeds
- ½ teaspoon ground cinnamon
- Pinch of ground ginger
- Pinch of ground nutmeg
- Pinch of ground cloves
- Pinch of salt
- 3 tablespoons honey
- 2 tablespoons coconut oil, melted
- ½ cup raisins

How to Prepare

1. Preheat your oven to 350°F.
2. Lightly grease a large baking sheet.
3. In a large bowl, add quinoa, coconut flakes, almonds, seeds, spices, and salt.
4. Add the honey and oil and stir until well blended.
5. Transfer the quinoa mixture onto the prepared baking sheet and spread in an even layer.
6. Bake for approximately 12–15 minutes, stirring after every 3–4 minutes.
7. Remove the baking sheet of granola from oven and set aside to cool completely before serving.
8. Break the granola into desired-sized chunks and serve with your favorite non-dairy milk.
9. You can preserve this granola in an airtight container.

Oats & Nuts Granola

Preparation time: 15 minutes

Cooking time: 25 minutes

Total time: 35 minutes

Servings: 20

Nutritional Values

Calories 218, Total Fat 10.5 g, Saturated Fat 1.6 g, Cholesterol 0 mg ,

Sodium 32 mg, Total Carbs 27.5 g, Fiber 4.7 g, Sugar 6.1 g, Protein 5.4 g

Ingredients

- ¼ cup applesauce
- ¼ cup canola oil
- 1½ teaspoons vanilla extract
- 6 cups old-fashioned rolled oats
- 2 cups bran flakes
- 1 cup almonds, slivered
- ¾ cup pecans, chopped
- ½ cup unsweetened coconut, shredded
- 1 cup raisins

How to Prepare

1. Preheat your oven to 325°F.
2. Lightly grease a baking sheet.
3. In a small pan, add applesauce, oil, and vanilla extract over low heat and cook for about 5 minutes, stirring occasionally.
4. Add remaining ingredients (except the raisins) and gently stir to combine.
5. Place the mixture onto the prepared baking sheet and spread in an even layer.
6. Bake for approximately 25 minutes or until granola becomes golden brown, stirring occasionally.
7. Remove the baking sheet of granola from oven and set aside to cool slightly.
8. Add raisins and stir to combine.
9. Set aside to cool completely.
10. Break the granola into desired-sized chunks and serve with your favorite non-dairy milk.
11. You can preserve this granola in an airtight container.

BAKED OATMEAL

Preparation time: 15 minutes

Cooking time: 30 minutes

Total time: 45 minutes

Servings: 4

Nutritional Values

Calories 263, Total Fat 9.3 g, Saturated Fat 3 g, Cholesterol 0 mg,

Sodium 295 mg, Total Carbs 21.6 g, Fiber 4.1 g, Sugar 7 g, Protein 23.8 g

Ingredients

- ¾ cup steel cut oats
- 1 scoop unsweetened protein powder
- 1 teaspoon ground cinnamon
- 1 teaspoon baking powder
- Pinch of sea salt
- 2 cups egg whites
- ½ cup unsweetened applesauce
- 1 cup unsweetened almond milk
- 2½ teaspoons coconut oil, melted
- 1 teaspoon vanilla extract
- 1/3 cup almonds, slivered
- 2/3 cup fresh blueberries

How to Prepare

1. Preheat your oven to 350°F.
2. Lightly, grease a 9x9-inch baking sheet.
3. In a bowl, add oats, protein powder, cinnamon, baking powder, and salt and mix well.
4. In a second bowl, add remaining ingredients (except for almonds and blueberries) and beat until well blended.
5. Add egg mixture into oats mixture and mix until well blended.
6. Fold in almonds and blueberries.
7. Place the oat mixture onto the prepared baking sheet and spread in an even layer.
8. Bake for approximately 30 minutes or until a wooden skewer inserted in the center comes out clean.
9. Serve warm.

Eggs in a Hole

Preparation time: 10 minutes

Cooking time: 9 minutes

Total time: 19 minutes

Servings: 4

Nutritional Values

Calories 232, Total Fat 12.7 g, Saturated Fat 4.1 g, Cholesterol 204 mg,

Sodium 545 mg, Total Carbs 13 g, Fiber 2.1 g, Sugar 2.2 g, Protein 16

Ingredients

- 2 bacon slices
- 4 (1-ounce) multigrain bread slices, lightly toasted
- 4 large eggs
- ¼ ounce pecorino Romano cheese, grated

How to Prepare

1. Preheat your oven to 400°F.
2. Arrange a rack in the middle portion of oven.
3. Place a jelly-roll pan in the oven while heating.
4. Place the bacon slice onto the heated pan and bake for approximately 4 minutes.
5. Remove from oven and crumble the bacon.
6. With a 3-inch biscuit cutter, cut a hole into the center of each bread slice.
7. Arrange bread slices onto the same jelly-roll pan.
8. Carefully crack 1 egg into each read hole.
9. Sprinkle the sides of each slice with crumbled bacon and cheese.
10. Bake for approximately 5 minutes or until egg whites are set.
11. Serve hot.

EGGS IN AVOCADO

Preparation time: 10 minutes

Cooking time: 20 minutes

Total time: 30 minutes

Servings: 4

Nutritional Values

Calories 375, Total Fat 32.4 g, Saturated Fat 9 g, Cholesterol 187 mg,

Sodium 446 mg, Total Carbs 9.3 g, Fiber 6.7 g, Sugar 0.9 g,Protein 14.6 g

Ingredients

- 2 ripe avocados, halved and pitted
- 4 eggs
- Salt and ground black pepper, as needed
- ¼ cup cheddar cheese, shredded
- 2 cooked bacon strips, crumbled

How to Prepare

1. Preheat the oven to 425°F.
2. With a spon, scoop out about 2 tablespoons of flesh from each half of avocado.
3. Arrange the avocado halves in a small baking dish.
4. In a small cup, break an egg and then carefully transfer into an avocado half.
5. Repeat with remaining eggs and sprinkle with salt and black pepper.
6. Bake for approximately 15–20 minutes or until desired doneness.
7. Serve immediately with the sprinkling of cheese and bacon.

CLOUD EGGS

Preparation time: 15 minutes

Cooking time: 10 minutes

Total time: 25 minutes

Servings: 2

Nutritional Values

Calories 130, Total Fat 2.5 g, Saturated Fat 1.5 g, Cholesterol 164 mg,

Sodium 309 mg, Total Carbs 13.1 g, Fiber 0.6 g, Sugar 1.4 g, Protein 7.5 g

Ingredients

- 2 eggs, separated
- Pinch of red pepper flakes, crushed
- Salt, as needed
- 1 teaspoon fresh chives, chopped
- 2 bread slices, toasted

How to Prepare

1. Preheat your oven to 350°F.
2. Line grease a baking sheet.
3. In a glass bowl, add the egg whites and with an electric mixer and beat until stiff peaks form.
4. With a spoon, place the egg whites onto the prepared baking sheet in 2 circles.
5. With the back of a spoon, make a hole in each egg white circle.
6. Bake for approximately 6 minutes.
7. Remove from oven and carefully place the egg yolks in the hole of each circle.
8. Sprinkle with red pepper flakes and salt.
9. Bake for approximately 3–4 minutes.
10. Serve hot with the garnishing of chives alongside the chives.

CAULIFLOWER TOAST WITH AVOCADO & EGGS

Preparation time: 15 minutes

Cooking time: 27 minutes

Total time: 42 minutes

Servings: 2

Nutritional Values

Calories 301, Total Fat 22.4 g,Saturated Fat 6.1 g,Cholesterol 251 mg,

Sodium 276 mg, Total Carbs 13 g, Fiber 7.9 g, Sugar 3.9 g, Protein 15.2 g

Ingredients

- 1 large egg
- 1 small head cauliflower, grated
- 1 medium avocado, pitted and chopped
- ¾ cup mozzarella cheese, shredded
- Salt and ground black pepper, as needed
- 2 fried eggs

How to Prepare

1. Preheat your oven to 420°F.
2. Line a baking sheet with parchment paper.
3. In a microwave-safe bowl, place the grated cauliflower and microwave on High for about 7 minutes.
4. Remove from microwave and place the cauliflower on paper towels to drain.
5. Gently squeeze the cauliflower to remove excess moisture.
6. Place the cauliflower in a bowl with mozzarella cheese, egg, salt, and black pepper and stir until well blended.
7. Arrange the cauliflower mixture onto the prepared baking sheet in two circles.
8. Bake for approximately 20 minutes or until golden brown on the edges.
9. Meanwhile, in a bowl, add avocado with a pinch of salt and black pepper and mash well.
10. Remove from oven and transfer the cauliflower toasts onto serving plates.
11. Spread the avocado onto the cauliflower toasts and top each with 1 egg.
12. Serve immediately.

CAULIFLOWER BAGELS

Preparation time: 15 minutes

Cooking time: 28 minutes

Total time: 43 minutes

Servings: 2

Nutritional Values

Calories 122, Total Fat 6.7 g, Saturated Fat 3.8 g, Cholesterol 63 mg,

Sodium 172 mg, Total Carbs 8.4 g, Fiber 3.8 g, Sugar 3.8 g, Protein 9.1 g

Ingredients

- ¼ cup sharp cheddar cheese, shredded
- 3 cups cauliflower florets, finely chopped
- ¼ cup mozzarella cheese, shredded
- 1¼ teaspoons everything bagel seasoning
- ½ large egg, lightly beaten

How to Prepare

1. Preheat your oven to 425°F.
2. Line a baking sheet with parchment paper.
3. In a microwave-safe bowl, add the chopped cauliflower and microwave on High for about 3 minutes.
4. Remove from microwave and place the cauliflower on paper towels to drain.
5. Set aside to cool slightly.
6. In a bowl, add the cauliflower, egg, and cheddar cheese until well blended.
7. Divide the mixture into 4 equal parts and transfer onto the prepared baking sheet.
8. With your hands, flatten each portion into 3½-inch circles.
9. With a 1-inch biscuit cutter, make a hole in the center of each circle.
10. Top each bagel with mozzarella cheese and sprinkle with bagel seasoning.
11. Bake for approximately 25 minutes or until browned around the edges.
12. Serve warm.

BLUEBERRY FRENCH TOAST

Preparation time: 15 minutes

Cooking time: 30 minutes

Total time: 45 minutes

Servings: 8

Nutritional Values

Calories 157, Total Fat 4.3 g, Saturated Fat 1.3 g, Cholesterol 117 mg

Sodium 240 mg, Total Carbs 22.9 g, Fiber 2.7 g, Sugar 11.4 g, Protein 7.7 g

Ingredients

- 8 (½-inch) whole-wheat bread slices
- 5 large eggs, beaten
- ¼ cup milk
- ¼ cup maple syrup
- ½ teaspoon ground cinnamon
- ¼ teaspoon salt
- 2 cups frozen blueberries, thawed

How to Prepare

1. Preheat the oven to 355°F.
2. Arrange a wire rack in the center of oven.
3. Grease a baking sheet.
4. In a bowl, add eggs, milk, maple syrup, cinnamon, and salt and beat until well blended.
5. Dip each bread slice in the egg mixture evenly.
6. Arrange the bread onto the prepared baking sheet in a single layer.
7. Set aside for about 5–10 minutes.
8. Top each bread slice with blueberries.
9. Bake for approximately 26–30 minutes or until bread slices becomes golden brown.
10. Serve hot.

Eggs in Zucchini Nest

Preparation time: 15 minutes

Cooking time: 20 minutes

Total time: 35 minutes

Servings: 4

Nutritional Values

Calories 161, Total Fat 11.1 g, Saturated Fat 3.7 g, Cholesterol 175 mg

Sodium 279 mg, Total Carbs 5.4 g, Fiber 1.1 g, Sugar 2.2 g, Protein 11.3 g

Ingredients

- 2 medium zucchinis, spiralized with blade C
- 1 tablespoon extra-virgin olive oil
- ¼ teaspoon garlic powder
- ¼ teaspoon salt
- ¼ teaspoon ground black pepper, divided
- ½ cup part-skim ricotta cheese
- 2 tablespoons Parmesan cheese, grated
- 4 medium eggs

How to Prepare

1. Preheat your oven to 400°F.
2. Grease a large rimmed baking sheet.
3. In a bowl, add zucchini, oil, garlic powder, salt, and 1/8 teaspoon of black pepper and toss to coat well.
4. Place 1 cup zucchini mixture onto the prepared baking sheet and shape it into a nest.
5. Repeat with remaining zucchini.
6. Bake for approximately 5 minutes.
7. Meanwhile, in a bowl, add ricotta, Parmesan, and remaining black pepper and mix well.
8. Remove the baking sheet of zucchini nest from oven and place the cheese mixture in the center of each.
9. With a spoon, create an indentation in the center of each nest.
10. Carefully crack an egg into each indentation.
11. Bake for approximately 12–15 minutes or until desired doneness of eggs.
12. Serve warm.

Eggs with Bacon & Brussels Sprouts

Preparation time: 15 minutes

Cooking time: 30 minutes

Total time: 45 minutes

Servings: 4

Nutritional Values

Calories 370, Total Fat 21.4 g, Saturated Fat 2.7 g, Cholesterol 93 mg

Sodium 316 mg, Total Carbs 35.4 g, Fiber 5.6 g, Sugar 27.6 g, Protein 5.1 g

Ingredients

- 2 garlic cloves, minced
- 2 tablespoons balsamic vinegar
- 1 tablespoon olive oil
- 1 tablespoon honey
- Salt and ground black pepper, as needed
- 2 pounds brussels sprouts, quartered
- 4 bacon slices, chopped
- 4 large eggs

How to Prepare

1. Preheat your oven to 400°F.
2. Lightly grease a baking sheet.
3. In a bowl, add garlic, vinegar, oil, honey, salt, and black pepper, and beat until well blended.
4. Add the Brussels sprouts and bacon and toss to coat well.
5. Place the Brussels sprouts mixture onto the prepared baking sheet and spread in an even layer.
6. Bake for approximately 10–12 minutes.
7. Remove the baking sheet of brussels sprout mixture from oven.
8. With a spoon, create 4 wells in the Brussels sprouts mixture.
9. Carefully crack 1 egg in each well.
10. Sprinkle eggs with salt and black pepper.
11. Bake for approximately 7–9 minutes or until desired doneness of eggs.
12. Serve hot.

HAM AND CHEESE POCKETS

Preparation time: 15 minutes

Cooking time: 21 minutes

Total time: 36 minutes

Servings: 2

Nutritional Values

Calories 358, Total Fat 26.8 g, Saturated Fat 12.8 g, Cholesterol 75 mg,

Sodium 1,002 mg, Total Carbs 7.3 g, Fiber 4.6 g, Sugar 0.3 g, Protein 25 g

Ingredients

- 1 ounce cream cheese
- ¾ cup mozzarella cheese, shredded
- 4 tablespoons flax meal
- 3 ounces provolone cheese slices
- 3 ounces ham

How to Prepare

1. Preheat your oven to 400°F.
2. Line a baking sheet with parchment paper.
3. In a microwave-safe bowl, add mozzarella cheese and cream cheese and microwave for about 1 minute.
4. Remove from microwave and stir in the flax meal until a dough forms.
5. Divide the dough in 2 portions.
6. With a rolling pan, roll each dough portion.
7. Arrange each rolled dough piece onto the prepared baking sheet.
8. Place the provolone cheese slices and ham on top of each dough portion on one side, then fold the other side over top.
9. With your fingers, pinch the edges of dough to seal.
10. Bake for approximately 20 minutes or until top becomes golden brown.
11. Remove the baking sheet of pockets from oven and set aside to cool slightly.
12. Cut each pocket in half while and serve.

BAKED STRAWBERRY PANCAKES

Preparation time: 15 minutes

Cooking time: 16 minutes

Total time: 31 minutes

Servings: 12

Nutritional Values

Calories 236, Total Fat 7.6 g, Saturated Fat 4 g, Cholesterol 63 mg

Sodium 602 mg, Total Carbs 35.6g, Fiber 2.5 g, Sugar 11.6 g, Protein 7.4 g

Ingredients
- 1 1/3 cups all-purpose flour
- 1 1/3 cups white whole-wheat flour
- 2¼ teaspoons baking powder
- 1¼ teaspoons baking soda
- 1 teaspoon kosher salt
- 3 cups low-fat buttermilk
- 3 large eggs
- ½ cup plus 1 tablespoon pure maple syrup
- ½ teaspoon almond extract
- 1/3 cup unsalted butter, melted
- 1¼ cups fresh strawberries, hulled and sliced thinly

How to Prepare
1. Preheat your oven to 500°F.
2. Lightly grease an 18x13-inch rimmed baking sheet.
3. In a bowl, place flours, baking powder, baking soda, and salt and mix well.
4. In a second bowl, add the buttermilk, eggs, 1 tablespoon of maple syrup, and almond extract and beat until well blended.
5. Add egg mixture into the bowl of flour mixture and mix until well blended.
6. Add the melted butter and gently stir to combine.
7. Set aside for about 5 minutes.
8. Place the pancake mixture onto the prepared baking sheet and spread in an even layer.
9. Arrange strawberry pieces on top.
10. Place the baking sheet in oven and immediately set the temperature to 425°F.
11. Bake for approximately 14–16 minutes or until a wooden skewer inserted in the center comes out clean.
12. Remove from oven and set aside for about 5 minutes.
13. Cut into 12 pieces and serve with the topping of remaining maple syrup.

HASH BROWN & BACON BAKE

Preparation time: 10 minutes

Cooking time: 37 minutes

Total time: 47 minutes

Servings: 6

Nutritional Values

Calories 689, Total Fat 51.7 g, Saturated Fat 17.6 g, Cholesterol 254 mg,

Sodium 940 mg, Total Carbs 34.7 g, Fiber 3.1 g, Sugar 2 g, Protein 21.2 g

Ingredients

- 2 tablespoons unsalted butter, melted
- 1 tablespoon olive oil
- ¼ teaspoon dried oregano
- ¼ teaspoon dried basil
- ¼ teaspoon dried thyme
- ¼ teaspoon garlic powder
- Salt and ground black pepper, as needed
- 1 cup cheddar cheese, shredded
- 1 (20-ounce) package refrigerated hash brown potatoes
- 12 bacon slices, chopped
- 6 large eggs
- 2 tablespoons fresh chives, chopped

How to Prepare

1. Preheat your oven to 400°F.
2. Lightly grease a baking sheet.
3. In a large bowl, add the butter, oil, herbs, garlic powder, salt, and black pepper and mix well.
4. Add the hash browns and gently toss to coat well.
5. In the bottom of prepared baking sheet, place hash browns in an even layer and sprinkle with cheese.
6. Bake for approximately 20–25 minutes.
7. Remove from oven and place the bacon pieces on top.
8. With a spoon, create 6 wells in the hash browns.
9. Carefully crack 1 egg in each well and sprinkle with salt and black pepper.
10. Bake for approximately 12 minutes.
11. Serve hot.

CHAPTER 3:

CHICKEN

RECIPES

HERBED SPATCHCOCK CHICKEN

Preparation time: 15 minutes

Cooking time: 50 minutes

Total time: 1 hour 5 minutes

Servings: 6

Nutritional Values

Calories 644, Total Fat 29.6 g, Saturated Fat 7.3 g, Cholesterol 269 mg,

Sodium 290 mg, Total Carbs 1.6 g, Fiber 0.5 g, Sugar 0.3 g, Protein 87.8 g

Ingredients

- 1 (4-pound) whole chicken, neck and giblets removed
- 1 (1-inch) piece fresh ginger piece, chopped
- 4 garlic cloves, chopped
- 1 small bunch fresh thyme
- 1 small bunch fresh rosemary
- ½ teaspoon paprika
- ½ teaspoon ground cumin
- Salt and ground black pepper, as needed
- ¼ cup fresh lemon juice
- 3 tablespoons olive oil

How to Prepare

1. Arrange the chicken onto a large cutting board, breast-side down.
2. With a kitchen shear, start from thigh and cut along one side of the backbone and turn chicken around.
3. Now, cut along the other side and discard the backbone.
4. Change the side and open it like a book.
5. Pound the backbone firmly to flatten.
6. Add the remaining ingredients (except for chicken) in a food processor and pulse until smooth.
7. In a large baking dish, add the marinade mixture.
8. Add chicken and coat with marinade generously.
9. With a plastic wrap, cover the baking dish and refrigerate to marinate for overnight.
10. Preheat your oven to 450°F.
11. Arrange a rack in a roasting pan.
12. Remove the chicken from refrigerator and discard the excess marinade.
13. Arrange the chicken onto the rack over roasting pan, skin side down.
14. Roast for approximately 25 minutes.
15. Flip the chicken and roast for about 25 minutes.
16. Remove the roasting pan of chicken from oven and place onto a platter for about 10 minutes before carving.
17. With a knife, cut the chicken into desired-sized pieces and serve.

CHICKEN WITH POTATOES & CARROTS

Preparation time: 15 minutes

Cooking time: 1½ hours

Total time: 1¾ hours

Servings: 6

Nutritional Values

Calories 722, Total Fat 30.9 g, Saturated Fat 7.4 g, Cholesterol 269 mg,

Sodium 319 mg, Total Carbs 17.5 g, Fiber 2.9 g, Sugar 2.8 g, Protein 89.4 g

Ingredients

- 1 (4-pound) whole chicken, neck and giblets removed
- Salt and ground black pepper, as needed
- 2 bunches fresh rosemary
- 1 lemon, halved
- 1 head garlic, halved
- ¼ cup olive oil
- 1 pound small potatoes
- ½ pound carrots, peeled and cut into chunks

How to Prepare

1. Preheat your oven to 400°F.
2. Season the cavity of chicken with salt and black pepper.
3. Then stuff the cavity with rosemary, lemon, and garlic.
4. Season the outer side of chicken with salt and black pepper generously.
5. With kitchen twine, tie the legs of the chicken together.
6. Arrange the chicken in a roasting pan, breast-side up.
7. Place the potatoes and carrot pieces around the chicken.
8. Drizzle the chicken and vegetables with oil evenly.
9. Roast for approximately 1–1½ hours, basting the chicken with the pan drippings after every 20 minutes.
10. Remove the baking sheet of chicken mixture from oven and place the chicken onto a platter for about 10 minutes before carving.
11. With a knife, cut the chicken into desired-sized pieces and serve alongside the vegetables.

ZESTY CHICKEN LEGS

Preparation time: 15 minutes

Cooking time: 50 minutes

Total time: 1 hour 5 minutes

Servings: 6

Nutritional Values

Calories 470, Total Fat 18.3 g, Saturated Fat 5.8 g, Cholesterol 202 mg,

Sodium 648 mg, Total Carbs 5.9 g, Fiber 1.3 g, Sugar 2.5 g, Protein 66.7 g

Ingredients

- 1 onion, chopped
- 1 tablespoon fresh turmeric, chopped
- 1–2 tablespoons fresh ginger, chopped
- 2 lemongrass stalks (bottom third), peeled and chopped
- 1–2 jalapeño peppers, seeded and chopped
- 1 teaspoon fresh lime zest, grated finely
- 1 tablespoon curry powder
- 1 teaspoon red pepper flakes, crushed
- 1¼ cups unsweetened coconut milk
- 3 tablespoons fresh lime juice
- 1 tablespoon soy sauce
- 1 tablespoon fish sauce
- 3 pounds chicken legs

How to Prepare

1. Add all ingredients (except for chicken legs) in a blender and pulse until smooth.
2. Transfer the mixture into a large roasting pan.
3. Add chicken legs and coat with marinade generously.
4. Cover and refrigerate to marinade for about 12 hours.
5. Remove chicken from refrigerator and set at room temperature for about 25–30 minutes before cooking.
6. Preheat your oven to 350°F.
7. Uncover the roasting pan and roast for about 50 minutes.
8. Serve hot.

GLAZED CHICKEN DRUMSTICKS

Preparation time: 15 minutes

Cooking time: 45 minutes

Total time: 1 hour

Servings: 8

Nutritional Values

Calories 405, Total Fat 10.3 g, Saturated Fat 2.6 g, Cholesterol 150 mg

Sodium 952 mg, Total Carbs 29.7 g, Fiber 0.5 g, Sugar 27.9 g ,Protein 48.5 g

Ingredients

Chicken Drumsticks

- ¾ cup honey
- ½ cup low-sodium soy sauce
- ¼ cup fresh orange juice
- 2 tablespoons Dijon mustard
- 1 tablespoon fresh ginger, grated finely
- 4 garlic cloves, crushed
- 8 skinless chicken drumsticks

Garnishing

- 2 teaspoons sesame seeds
- 2 scallions (green part), chopped

How to Prepare

1. Add all ingredients (except for drumsticks) in a bowl and beat until well blended.
2. Reserve about 2/3 cup of marinade in another small bowl and reserve in refrigerator.
3. In a large Ziploc bag, lace remaining marinade and drumsticks.
4. Seal the bag and shake to coat well.
5. Refrigerate overnight, shaking the bag occasionally.
6. Preheat your oven to 400°F.
7. Arrange a wire rack in the center of oven.
8. Line a baking sheet with parchment paper.
9. Arrange the chicken drumsticks onto the prepared baking sheet in a single layer, skin-side up.
10. Bake for approximately 55 minutes, flipping once after 25 minutes.
11. Meanwhile, place the reserved marinade into a small saucepan over medium heat and bring to a boil.
12. Immediately adjust the heat to low and simmer for about 7 minutes or until thickened.
13. Remove the baking sheet of chicken from oven and transfer onto a platter.
14. Coat the chicken drumsticks with glaze and serve with the garnishing of sesame seeds and scallion greens.

SPICED CHICKEN DRUMSTICKS

Preparation time: 10 minutes

Cooking time: 45 minutes

Total time: 55 minutes

Servings: 6

Nutritional Values

Calories 298, Total Fat 10.4 g, Saturated Fat 2.7 g, Cholesterol 150 mg,

Sodium 164 mg, Total Carbs 1 g, Fiber 0.5 g, Sugar 0.1 goProtein 47 g

Ingredients

- 2 tablespoons avocado oil
- 1 tablespoon dried rosemary, crushed
- 1 teaspoon garlic powder
- ½ teaspoon ground cumin
- Salt and ground black pepper, as needed
- 6 (6-ounce) chicken drumsticks

How to Prepare

1. In a large bowl, add the oil, rosemary, and spices and mix until well blended.
2. Add the chicken drumsticks and coat with the mixture generously.
3. Set aside at room temperature for about 20–30 minutes.
4. Preheat your oven to 425°F.
5. Grease a baking sheet.
6. Arrange the chicken drumsticks onto the prepared baking sheet in a single layer.
7. Bake for approximately 40–45 minutes, flipping once halfway through.
8. Serve immediately.

Chicken Drumsticks with Grapes

Preparation time: 15 minutes

Cooking time: 35 minutes

Total time: 50 minutes

Servings: 4

Nutritional Values

Calories 297, Total Fat 11.7 g, Saturated Fat 2.7 g, Cholesterol 125 mg,

Sodium 152 mg, Total Carbs 7 g, Fiber 0.4 g, Sugar 5.8 g, Protein 39.3 g

Ingredients

- 4 (5-ounce) chicken drumsticks
- 3 teaspoons olive oil, divided
- 1½ teaspoons fresh rosemary, chopped
- Salt and ground black pepper, as needed
- 1 cup red seedless grapes

How to Prepare

1. Preheat your oven to 425°F.
2. Line a baking sheet with a foil piece.
3. In a bowl, place chicken, 2 teaspoons of oil, rosemary, salt, and black pepper and toss to coat well.
4. Arrange the chicken drumsticks onto the prepared baking sheet.
5. Roast for approximately 10 minutes.
6. Meanwhile, in a bowl, place grapes, remaining oil, and a pinch of salt and toss to coat well.
7. Remove the baking sheet from oven and arrange the grapes around chicken drumsticks.
8. Roast for approximately 25 minutes.
9. Serve hot.

TERIYAKI CHICKEN THIGHS

Preparation time: 10 minutes

Cooking time: 40 minutes

Total time: 50 minutes

Servings: 8

Nutritional Values

Calories 302, Total Fat 12.5 g, Saturated Fat 3 g, Cholesterol 82 mg

Sodium 638 mg, Total Carbs 12.5 g, Fiber 0.2 g, Sugar 11.5 g, Protein 32.8 g

Ingredients

- ½ cup rice vinegar
- 5 tablespoons honey
- 1/3 cup low-sodium soy sauce
- ¼ cup sesame oil, toasted
- 3 tablespoons chili garlic sauce
- 3 tablespoons garlic, minced
- Ground black pepper, as needed
- 8 skinless, boneless chicken thighs
- 1 tablespoon sesame seeds

How to Prepare

1. Add all ingredients (except for chicken thighs and sesame seeds) in a bowl and beat until well blended.
2. Add half of the marinade and chicken thighs in a large Ziplock bag.
3. Seal the bag and shake to coat well.
4. Refrigerate for at least 1 hour, shaking the bag twice.
5. Reserve remaining marinade in the refrigerator until using.
6. Preheat your oven to 425°F.
7. In a small pan, add reserved marinade over medium heat and bring to a boil.
8. Cook for about 3–5 minutes, stirring occasionally.
9. Remove the pan of marinade from heat and set aside to cool slightly.
10. Remove the chicken thighs from Ziplock bag and discard the excess marinade.
11. Arrange the chicken thighs onto a baking sheet in a single layer and coat with 1/3 of the cooked marinade.
12. Bake for approximately 30 minutes, coating with the cooked marinade slightly after every 10 minutes.
13. Remove from oven and set aside for about 10 minutes.
14. Serve hot with the garnishing of sesame seeds.

GLAZED CHICKEN THIGHS

Preparation time: 15 minutes

Cooking time: 40 minutes

Total time: 55 minutes

Servings: 8

Nutritional Values

Calories 384, Total Fat 18.2 g, Saturated Fat 4.3 g, Cholesterol 151 mg

Sodium 452 mg, Total Carbs 2.9 g, Fiber 0.5 g, Sugar 1.8 g, Protein 49.6 g

Ingredients

- ½ of small apple, peeled, cored, and chopped
- 1 bunch scallion, trimmed and chopped roughly
- 1 teaspoon fresh ginger, chopped
- 2 garlic cloves, chopped
- 3 tablespoons olive oil
- ½ teaspoon sesame oil, toasted
- 3 tablespoons apple cider vinegar
- 1 tablespoon fish sauce
- 1 tablespoon low-sodium soy sauce
- Salt and ground black pepper, as needed
- 8 (6-ounce) chicken thighs

How to Prepare

1. Add all ingredients (except for chicken thighs) in a blender and pulse until smooth.
2. Place the mixture and chicken thighs into a large Ziploc bag.
3. Tightly seal the bag and shake to coat well.
4. Refrigerate to marinade for about 12 hours.
5. Preheat your oven to 400°F.
6. Arrange a rack onto a foil-lined baking sheet.
7. Place the chicken thighs onto the prepared baking sheet, skin-side down.
8. Roast for approximately 40 minutes, flipping once halfway through.
9. Serve hot.

STUFFED CHICKEN BREAST

Preparation time: 15 minutes

Cooking time: 24 minutes

Total time: 39 minutes

Servings: 4

Nutritional Values

Calories 211, Total Fat 10.5 g, Saturated Fat 3.5g, Cholesterol 74 mg

Sodium 260 mg, Total Carbs 1.9 g, Fiber 0.6 g, Sugar 0.7 g, Protein 27 g

Ingredients

- 4 (4-ounce) skinless, boneless chicken breast halves, pounded into ½-inch thickness
- Sea salt and fresh ground pepper, as needed
- ¼ cup Kalamata olives, pitted and chopped
- ¼ cup oil-packed sun-dried tomatoes, drained
- ¼ cup feta cheese, crumbled
- 1 tablespoon fresh dill, chopped
- 1 tablespoon fresh parsley, chopped
- 1 tablespoon extra-virgin olive oil

How to Prepare

1. Preheat your oven to 375°F.
2. Grease a rimmed baking sheet.
3. Rub the chicken with salt and black pepper.
4. In a large bowl, mix together olives, tomatoes, feta cheese, scallion, dill, and parsley.
5. Place chicken breast onto a cutting board.
6. Stuff the chicken breasts with the olive mixture and tightly roll up.
7. Secure each breast roll with toothpicks.
8. In a wok, heat oil over medium heat and cook breast rolls for about 2 minutes per side.
9. Remove from the heat and arrange the chicken rolls onto the prepared baking sheet in a single layer.
10. Bake for approximately 16–20 minutes or until desired doneness.
11. Remove the baking sheet from oven and set aside for about 5 minutes.
12. With a sharp knife, cut into desired-sized slices and serve.

PESTO CHICKEN

Preparation time: 15 minutes

Cooking time: 30 minutes

Total time: 45 minutes

Servings: 6

Nutritional Values

Calories 558, Total Fat 43.6 g, Saturated Fat 6.3 g, Cholesterol 101 mg,

Sodium 400 mg, Total Carbs 5 g, Fiber 2.7 g, Sugar 0.4 g, Protein 40.2 g

Ingredients

Pesto
- 3 cups fresh basil leaves
- 2 cups fresh baby spinach leaves
- 4 garlic cloves, peeled
- 1 cup raw walnuts
- 2/3 cup olive oil
- 2 tablespoons nutritional yeast
- ¾ teaspoon salt

Chicken
- 1½ pounds boneless, skinless chicken breasts
- Salt and ground black pepper, as needed
- Pinch of nutritional yeast
- 1 teaspoon Italian seasoning

How to Prepare

1. Preheat your oven to 400°F.
2. Generously grease a baking sheet.
3. **For pesto:** add all ingredients in a food processor and pulse until smooth.
4. Transfer the pesto into a bowl and refrigerate before using.
5. Sprinkle the chicken breasts with salt and black pepper evenly.
6. Arrange the chicken breasts into the prepared baking dish in a single layer.
7. Place the pesto over each breast evenly, reserving any remaining.
8. Sprinkle with nutritional yeast and Italian seasoning.
9. Bake for approximately 25–30 minutes or until done completely. Serve hot.

PARMESAN CHICKEN BREASTS

Preparation time: 10 minutes

Cooking time: 25 minutes

Total time: 35 minutes

Servings: 4

Nutritional Values

Calories 194, Total Fat 10.5 g, Saturated Fat 5.6 g, Cholesterol 83 mg,

Sodium 124 mg, Total Carbs 0.4 g, Fiber 0.1 g, Sugar 0 g, Protein 26.4 g

Ingredients

- 4 (4-ounce) skinless, boneless chicken breast halves
- 2 tablespoons unsalted butter, melted
- 2 tablespoon Parmesan cheese, shredded
- 1 garlic clove, minced
- ¼ cup fresh basil, minced
- Ground black pepper, as needed

How to Prepare

1. Preheat your oven to 325°F.
2. Lightly grease a rimmed baking sheet.
3. With a fork, pierce each chicken breast at several places.
4. In a bowl, combine the remaining ingredients.
5. Arrange the chicken breasts onto prepared baking sheet in a single layer.
6. Place the butter mixture over chicken breasts evenly.
7. Bake for approximately 25 minutes, basting with the pan juices after every 10 minutes.
8. Serve hot.

CHICKEN & BROCCOLI BAKE

Preparation time: 15 minutes

Cooking time: 30 minutes

Total time: 45 minutes

Servings: 6

Nutritional Values

Calories 333, Total Fat 10.5 g, Saturated Fat 2.7 g, Cholesterol 118 mg

Sodium 313 mg, Total Carbs 19.1 g, Fiber 1.6 g, Sugar 16.3 g, Protein 4.1 g

Ingredients

- 1/3 cup honey
- 1/3 cup Dijon mustard
- 1 teaspoon dried basil, crushed
- ¼ teaspoon ground turmeric
- Salt and ground black pepper, as needed
- 1¾ pounds chicken breasts
- 1 head broccoli, cut into small florets

How to Prepare

1. Preheat your oven to 350°F.
2. Lightly grease a large baking sheet.
3. In a bowl, add honey, mustard, basil, turmeric, salt, and black pepper and mix well.
4. Place chicken breasts onto the prepared baking sheet in a single layer.
5. Arrange the broccoli florets around the chicken evenly.
6. Place half of honey mixture over chicken and broccoli evenly.
7. Bake for approximately 20 minutes.
8. Remove the baking dish from oven.
9. Coat the chicken breasts with remaining honey mixture and bake for approximately 10 minutes more.

Spicy Chicken Leg Quarters

Preparation time: 10 minutes

Cooking time: 53 minutes

Total time: 1 hour 3 minutes

Servings: 3

Nutritional Values

Calories 725, Total Fat 59.7 g, Saturated Fat 12.9 g, Cholesterol 228 mg

Sodium 746 mg, Total Carbs 0.7 g, Fiber 0.3 g, Sugar 0.2 g, Protein 48.3 g

Ingredients

- 3 (10–11-ounce) bone-in, skin-on chicken leg quarters
- ½ cup mayonnaise
- 1 teaspoon paprika
- ½ teaspoon garlic powder
- Salt and ground white pepper, as needed

How to Prepare

1. Preheat your oven to 350°F.
2. Grease a roasting pan.
3. In a shallow bowl, place the mayonnaise.
4. In a bowl, combine the spices, salt, and white pepper.
5. Coat each chicken quarter with mayonnaise and then sprinkle evenly with the spice mixture.
6. Arrange the chicken quarters into prepared roasting pan in a single layer.
7. Bake for approximately 45 minutes.
8. Now, adjust the temperature of oven to 400°F.
9. Bake for approximately 5–8 minutes more.
10. Remove from oven and place the chicken quarters onto a platter.
11. With a piece of foil, cover each chicken quarter loosely for about 5 minutes before serving.

CHICKEN SAUSAGE WITH BRUSSELS SPROUTS

Preparation time: 15 minutes

Cooking time: 30 minutes

Total time: 45 minutes

Servings: 6

Nutritional Values

Calories 309, Total Fat 18.3 g, Saturated Fat 5.9 g, Cholesterol 136 mg

Sodium 900 mg, Total Carbs 19.9 g, Fiber 4.5 g, Sugar 4.7 g, Protein 19.4 g

Ingredients

- 1½ pounds Brussels sprouts, trimmed and halved
- 2 teaspoons olive oil, divided
- 2 teaspoons smoked paprika, divided
- Salt and ground black pepper, as needed
- 1½ pounds smoked chicken sausage, sliced

How to Prepare

1. Preheat your oven to 400°F.
2. Lightly grease a large baking sheet.
3. In a bowl, add Brussels sprouts, 1 teaspoon of oil, 1 teaspoon of paprika, salt, and black pepper and toss to coat well.
4. Place the Brussels sprouts onto the prepared baking sheet and spread in an even layer.
5. Roast for approximately 15 minutes.
6. Meanwhile, in a bowl, add the sausage slices, sausage with remaining oil, paprika, and black pepper and toss to coat well.
7. Remove from oven and push the Brussels sprouts to 1 side of the baking sheet.
8. Arrange the sausage slices onto another side of baking sheet.
9. Roast for approximately 15 minutes.
10. Serve hot.

CHICKEN KIEV

Preparation time: 20 minutes

Cooking time: 17 minutes

Total time: 37 minutes

Servings: 8

Nutritional Values

Calories 872, Total Fat 70.3 g, Saturated Fat 18.8 g, Cholesterol 130 mg

Sodium 138 mg, Total Carbs 16.5 g, Fiber 0.6 g, Sugar 0.2 g, Protein 29.2 g

Ingredients

- 2 garlic cloves, minced
- Salt, as needed
- 2 tablespoons fresh flat-leaf parsley, chopped
- 6 tablespoons unsalted butter
- 4 (8-ounce) skinless, boneless chicken breast halves, pounded into ¼-inch thickness
- Ground black pepper, as needed
- 1 cup all-purpose flour
- 2 eggs, beaten
- 2 cups panko breadcrumbs
- 2 cups vegetable oil
- Pinch of cayenne pepper

How to Prepare

1. With a mortar and pestle, grind garlic with a pinch of salt until garlic is completely smashed.
2. Add parsley and mix until completely combined.
3. Add butter and with mortar and pestle, mix until well blended.
4. With a plastic wrap, wrap the butter and refrigerate for at least 15 minutes.
5. Sprinkle the chicken breasts with salt and black pepper.
6. Place ¼ of the butter mixture in the center of each chicken breast.
7. Carefully fold the narrower end of each chicken breast up over the butter to form a tight pocket.
8. Then gather the sides of each chicken breast to the center to shape into a ball.
9. With a plastic wrap, cover each chicken breast ball tightly and arrange onto a large plate.

10. Freeze for about 30 minutes.
11. In a shallow dish, add flour and 2 teaspoons of salt and mix well.
12. Add eggs in a second shallow dish and with a wire whisk, beat well.
13. In a third shallow dish, put the panko breadcrumbs.
14. Remove the chicken breast balls from plastic wrap.
15. Coat each chicken breast ball with flour mixture, then dip into beaten eggs and finally coat with breadcrumbs and cayenne pepper.
16. Arrange the breaded chicken balls onto a plate.
17. With a plastic wrap, cover the plate and freeze for about 15 minutes.
18. Preheat your oven to 400°F.
19. Line a baking sheet with a foil piece.
20. In a large, deep skillet, heat the oil over medium heat and cook the chicken balls for about 1 minute per side.
21. With a slotted spoon, transfer the chicken balls onto the prepared baking sheet.
22. Sprinkle the chicken balls with salt and cayenne pepper.
23. Bake for approximately 15–17 minutes.
24. Remove the baking sheet from oven and set aside for about 5 minutes before serving.
25. Cut each chicken piece in half and serve.

CHAPTER 4:

VEGETARIAN MEALS RECIPES

ROASTED TOMATOES

Preparation time: 15 minutes

Cooking time: 20 minutes

Total time: 35 minutes

Servings: 6

Nutritional Values

Calories 80, Total Fat 5.2 g, Saturated Fat 0.8 g, Cholesterol 0 mg

Sodium 37 mg, Total Carbs 8.7 g, Fiber 2.8 g, Sugar 5 g, Protein 1.9 g

Ingredients

- 6 large tomatoes, halved
- Salt, as needed
- 2 tablespoons onion, chopped finely
- 3 garlic cloves, minced
- 1 jalapeño pepper, seeded and minced
- 1 tablespoon fresh rosemary, minced
- 1 teaspoon fresh thyme, minced
- 1 teaspoon fresh oregano, minced
- Ground black pepper, as needed
- 2 tablespoons extra-virgin olive oil

How to Prepare

1. Line a large tray with a kitchen towel.
2. Sprinkle the tomatoes with a little salt.
3. Arrange tomatoes onto the prepared plate, cut side down and set aside for about 30–40 minutes to drain completely.
4. Preheat your oven to 425°F.
5. Grease a baking sheet.
6. In a mixing bowl, mix together the onion, garlic, jalapeño pepper, herbs, and black pepper.
7. Arrange the tomatoes onto the prepared baking sheet in a single layer, cut side up.
8. Top each tomato half with herb mixture evenly and drizzle with oil generously.
9. Roast for approximately 20 minutes.
10. Serve warm.

HERBED POTATOES

Preparation time: 15 minutes

Cooking time: 35 minutes

Total time: 50 minutes

Servings: 6

Nutritional Values

Calories 149, Total Fat 4.9 g, Saturated Fat 0.7 g, Cholesterol 0 mg,

Sodium 9 mg, Total Carbs 24.9 g, Fiber 2.9 g, Sugar 1.7 g, Protein 3.1 g

Ingredients

- 2 pounds red potatoes, scrubbed and cubed
- 2 tablespoons olive oil
- 1 teaspoon garlic powder
- 3 tablespoons fresh herbs (rosemary, parsley, thyme, basil), chopped
- ½ teaspoon paprika
- Salt and ground black pepper, as needed

How to Prepare

1. In a bowl of water, place potato cubes and soaks for up to 1 hour.
2. Preheat your oven to 425°F.
3. Lightly grease a large baking sheet.
4. Drain the potatoes and with paper towels, then completely pat them dry.
5. In a bowl, place potatoes, olive oil, herbs, paprika, salt, and black pepper and toss to coat well.
6. Arrange the potato cubes onto the prepared baking sheet and spread in an even layer.
7. Bake for approximately 30–35 minutes or until tender.
8. Serve hot.

Parmesan Brussels Sprouts

Preparation time: 10 minutes

Cooking time: 20 minutes

Total time: 30 minutes

Servings: 2

Nutritional Values

Calories 201, Total Fat 5.2 g, Saturated Fat 5 g, Cholesterol 20 mg

Sodium 269 mg, Total Carbs 11 g, Fiber 4.4 g, Sugar 2.5 g, Protein 13 g

Ingredients

- 8 ounces Brussels sprouts
- 1 tablespoon olive oil
- ½ teaspoon dried rosemary
- Salt and ground black pepper, as needed
- 2 ounces Parmesan cheese, shredded

How to Prepare

1. Preheat your oven to 450°F.
2. Grease a baking sheet.
3. In a bowl, add the Brussels sprouts, oil, rosemary, salt, and black pepper and toss to coat well.
4. Arrange the Brussels sprouts onto the prepared baking sheet in a single layer and sprinkle with Parmesan cheese.
5. Roast for approximately 20 minutes.
6. Serve hot.

BUTTERED ASPARAGUS

Preparation time: 10 minutes

Cooking time: 25 minutes

Total time: 35 minutes

Servings: 3

Nutritional Values

Calories 74, Total Fat 5.9 g, Saturated Fat 3.7 g, Cholesterol 15 mg

Sodium 94 mg, Total Carbs 4.4 g, Fiber 2.4 g, Sugar 2.1 g, Protein 2.6 g

Ingredients

- 1½ tablespoons butter, melted
- ¾ pound asparagus stalks, trimmed
- Salt and ground black pepper, as needed

How to Prepare

1. Preheat your oven to 400°F.
2. Lightly grease a baking sheet.
3. Place the asparagus stalks onto the prepared baking sheet and drizzle with olive oil.
4. Sprinkle with salt and black pepper.
5. Bake for approximately 25 minutes.
6. Serve hot.

PARMESAN BROCCOLI

Preparation time: 10 minutes

Cooking time: 18 minutes

Total time: 28 minutes

Servings: 2

Nutritional Values

Calories 118, Total Fat 8.9 g, Saturated Fat 2.1 g, Cholesterol 5 mg

Sodium 96 mg, Total Carbs 7.3 g, Fiber 0.4 g, Sugar 0.3 g, Protein 5.8 g

Ingredients

- 1 tablespoon olive oil
- 2 tablespoons Parmesan cheese, grated
- ½ (16-ounce) bag frozen broccoli florets
- Salt and black pepper, as needed
- ½ of medium lemon, sliced

How to Prepare

1. Preheat your oven to 450°F.
2. Lightly grease a baking sheet.
3. In a bowl, place broccoli, olive oil, salt, and black pepper and toss to coat.
4. Arrange the broccoli florets onto the prepared baking sheet in a single layer.
5. Bake for approximately 15 minutes.
6. Remove from the oven and arrange lemon slices over broccoli.
7. Sprinkle the top with Parmesan cheese.
8. Bake for approximately 2–3 minutes or until cheese melts completely.
9. Serve hot.

ROASTED BUTTERNUT SQUASH

Preparation time: 10 minutes

Cooking time: 45 minutes

Total time: 55 minutes

Servings: 6

Nutritional Values

Calories 99, Total Fat 4 g, Saturated Fat 2.5 g, Cholesterol 10 mg

Sodium 61 mg, Total Carbs 16.9 g, Fiber 3 g, Sugar 3.1 g, Protein 1.5 g

Ingredients

- 2 tablespoons butter, melted
- ½ teaspoon ground cumin
- ½ teaspoon ground cinnamon
- ¼ teaspoon red pepper flakes, crushed
- Salt, as needed
- 6¼ cups butternut squash, peeled, seeded and cut into equal-sized cubes
- 3 tablespoons fresh cilantro leaves, chopped

How to Prepare

1. Preheat your oven to 425°F.
2. Line 2 large baking sheets with pieces of foil.
3. In a bowl, add and toss to coat well.
4. Arrange the squash pieces onto the prepared baking sheets in a single layer.
5. Roast for approximately 40–45 minutes.
6. Serve hot with the garnishing of cilantro.

THYME BOK CHOY

Preparation time: 10 minutes

Cooking time: 1 hour

Total time: 1 hour 10 minutes

Servings: 6

Nutritional Values

Calories 102, Total Fat 8.8 g, Saturated Fat 1.2 g, Cholesterol 0 mg

Sodium 144 mg, Total Carbs 5.6 g, Fiber 2.6 g, Sugar 2.2 g, Protein 2.2 g

Ingredients

- 2 large cauliflower heads
- 2 garlic cloves, halved
- ¼ cup olive oil
- 3 tablespoons Dijon mustard
- Salt and ground black pepper, as needed
- ¼ cup fresh parsley, chopped

How to Prepare

1. Preheat your oven to 450°F.
2. Arrange a rack in the bottom position of the oven.
3. Line a baking sheet with a foil piece.
4. Remove the leaves from each cauliflower head and then trim the stem.
5. Rub the outside of each cauliflower head with the cut garlic.
6. In a bowl, add the oil, mustard, salt, and black pepper and mix well.
7. Arrange the cauliflower heads onto the prepared baking sheet and brush the outside and inside with the oil mixture.
8. Roast for approximately 50–60 minutes.
9. Remove the baking sheet of cauliflower from oven and set aside for about 2–3 minutes before serving.
10. Serve with the garnishing of parsley.

LEMONY CABBAGE

Preparation time: 10 minutes

Cooking time: 30 minutes

Total time: 40 minutes

Servings: 4

Nutritional Values

Calories 76, Total Fat 3.7 g, Saturated Fat 0.6 g, Cholesterol 0 mg

Sodium 72 mg, Total Carbs 10.5 g, Fiber 4.5 g, Sugar 5.8 g, Protein 2.3 g

Ingredients

- 1 green cabbage head, cut into 8 wedges
- 1½ tablespoons fresh lemon juice
- 1 tablespoon olive oil
- Salt and ground black pepper, as needed

How to Prepare

1. Preheat your oven to 450°F.
2. Lightly grease a baking sheet.
3. In a bowl, add lemon juice, oil, salt, and black pepper and mix well.
4. Coat the cabbage wedges with the oil mixture evenly.
5. Arrange the cabbage wedges onto the prepared baking sheet in a single layer.
6. Roast for approximately 30 minutes, flipping once halfway through.
7. Serve hot.

GLAZED BABY CARROTS

Preparation time: 10 minutes

Cooking time: 30 minutes

Total time: 40 minutes

Servings: 6

Nutritional Values

Calories 152, Total Fat 8.8 g, Saturated Fat 3.2 g, Cholesterol 10 mg

Sodium 173 mg, Total Carbs 18.8 g, Fiber 4.4 g, Sugar 13 g, Protein 1.1 g

Ingredients

- 2 tablespoons olive oil
- 2 tablespoons butter, melted
- 2 tablespoons honey
- 3 garlic cloves, minced
- ½ teaspoon Italian seasoning
- Salt and ground black pepper, as needed
- 2 pounds fresh baby carrots
- 2 teaspoons fresh parsley, chopped

How to Prepare

1. Preheat your oven to 425°F.
2. Lightly grease a large-rimmed baking sheet.
3. In a large bowl, add the oil, butter, honey, garlic, Italian seasoning, salt, and black pepper and beat until combined.
4. Add the carrots and toss to coat.
5. Arrange the carrots onto the prepared baking sheet in a single layer.
6. Bake for approximately 25–30 minutes or until carrots are fork-tender.
7. Serve immediately with the garnishing of parsley.

GREEN BEANS WITH CARROTS

Preparation time: 15 minutes

Cooking time: 30 minutes

Total time: 45 minutes

Servings: 5

Nutritional Values

Calories 94, Total Fat 5.8 g, Saturated Fat 0.9 g, Cholesterol 0 mg

Sodium 75 mg, Total Carbs 10.7 g, Fiber 3.7 g, Sugar 3.7 g, Protein 1.7 g

Ingredients

- 10 ounces carrots, peeled and cut into 2-inch sticks
- 10 ounces fresh green beans, trimmed and halved
- 2 tablespoons olive oil
- 1 tablespoon fresh lemon juice
- 1 tablespoon fresh rosemary, minced
- 3 garlic cloves, minced
- Salt and ground black pepper, as needed

How to Prepare

1. Preheat your oven to 400°F.
2. Lightly grease a large baking sheet.
3. In a bowl, add vegetables, oil, lemon juice, rosemary, garlic, salt, and black pepper and toss to coat well.
4. Arrange the carrot mixture onto the prepared baking sheet in a single layer.
5. Bake for approximately 25–30 minutes, stirring once halfway through.
6. Serve hot.

CHEESY ZUCCHINI

Preparation time: 15 minutes

Cooking time: 23 minutes

Total time: 38 minutes

Servings: 4

Nutritional Values

Calories 251, Total Fat 7.5 g, Saturated Fat 3.5 g, Cholesterol 104 mg

Sodium 294 mg, Total Carbs 20.1 g, Fiber 2.3 g, Sugar 4.8 g, Protein 10.4 g

Ingredients

- 1/3 cup all-purpose flour
- 2 large eggs
- 1 cup panko breadcrumbs
- 1/3 cup Parmesan cheese, grated freshly
- Salt and ground black pepper, as needed
- 2 zucchinis, cut into ¼-inch-thick rounds
- ½ cup marinara sauce
- ½ cup mozzarella pearls, drained
- 2 tablespoons fresh parsley leaves, chopped

How to Prepare

1. Preheat your oven to 400°F.
2. Lightly grease a large baking sheet.
3. In a shallow dish, place the flour.
4. Crack the eggs in a second shallow bowl and whisk them.
5. In a third shallow dish, combine the panko, Parmesan, salt, and black pepper.
6. Coat the zucchini rounds with flour, then dip into eggs and finally coat with panko mixture.
7. Arrange the zucchini rounds onto the prepared baking sheet in a single layer.
8. Bake for approximately 18–20 minutes or until tender and golden brown.
9. Remove the baking sheet of zucchini rounds from the oven and top with marinara sauce, followed by the mozzarella cheese.
10. Now, set the oven to boiler.
11. Broil for approximately 2–3 minutes or until the cheese is melted.
12. Serve immediately with the garnishing of parsley.

STUFFED BELL PEPPERS

Preparation time: 15 minutes

Cooking time: 25 minutes

Total time: 40 minutes

Servings: 4

Nutritional Values

Calories 288, Total Fat 21.4 g, Saturated Fat 3.6 g, Cholesterol 15 mg

Sodium 286 mg, Total Carbs 19.9 g, Fiber 4.3 g, Sugar 8.7 g, Protein 9.6 g

Ingredients

- ½ pound fresh shiitake mushrooms
- 1 cup celery stalk
- 2 garlic cloves, peeled
- ½ cup walnuts, chopped
- 2 tablespoons olive oil
- Salt and ground black pepper, as needed
- 4 small bell peppers, halved and seeded
- ½ cup cheddar cheese, shredded

How to Prepare

1. Preheat your oven to 400°F.
2. Grease a large baking sheet.
3. In a food processor, add mushrooms, celery, garlic, walnuts, oil, salt, and pepper and pulse until chopped finely.
4. Stuff the bell peppers with mushroom mixture and sprinkle with cheese.
5. Arrange the bell peppers onto the prepared baking sheet.
6. Bake for approximately 20–25 minutes.
7. Serve hot.

GLAZED TOFU

Preparation time: 15 minutes

Cooking time: 30 minutes

Total time: 45 minutes

Servings: 4

Nutritional Values

Calories 185, Total Fat 13.4 g, Saturated Fat 1.6 g, Cholesterol 0 mg

Sodium 508 mg, Total Carbs 6.6 g, Fiber 0.5 g, Sugar 3.7 g, Protein 11.8 g

Ingredients

- 2 tablespoons soy sauce
- 2 tablespoons sesame oil
- 1 tablespoon rice vinegar
- 3 teaspoons maple syrup
- 1 teaspoon sriracha
- Pinch of onion powder
- Pinch of garlic powder
- Pinch of salt
- 1 pound extra-firm tofu, pressed, drained and cut into 1-inch slabs

How to Prepare

1. Preheat your oven to 400°F.
2. Grease a baking sheet.
3. In a bowl, add soy sauce, sesame oil, vinegar, maple syrup, sriracha, onion powder, garlic powder, and salt and beat until well blended.
4. Add tofu pieces and coat with mixture generously.
5. Arrange tofu pieces onto the prepared baking sheet in a single layer.
6. Bake for approximately 30 minutes, flipping once halfway through.
7. Serve warm.

QUINOA BURGERS

Preparation time: 20 minutes

Cooking time: 50 minutes

Total time: 1 hour 10 minutes

Servings: 4

Nutritional Values

Calories 355, Total Fat 23.6 g, Saturated Fat 5.9 g, Cholesterol 66 mg

Sodium 361 mg, Total Carbs 25.2 g, Fiber 4.9 g, Sugar 2.9 g, Protein 13.5 g

Ingredients

- 1 cup water
- ½ cup red quinoa, rinsed
- 1 tablespoon canola oil
- 1 cup onion, chopped
- 2 cups fresh button mushrooms, chopped finely
- 1 teaspoon garlic, minced
- ¾ teaspoon dried marjoram, crushed
- ¼ teaspoon dried oregano, crushed
- 2/3 cup cheddar cheese, shredded
- 1 large egg, beaten
- ½ cup pecans, toasted and chopped finely
- 1/3 cup quick-cooking rolled oats
- 1 tablespoon low-sodium soy sauce

How to Prepare

1. In a medium pan, add water and quinoa over medium-high heat and bring to a boil.
2. Adjust the heat to low and simmer, covered and for about 15 minutes.
3. Remove the pan of quinoa from heat and set aside, covered for about 10 minutes.
4. Uncover the pan and with a fork, fluff the quinoa.
5. Set aside to cool completely.
6. Meanwhile, in a large pan, heat oil over medium heat and sauté the onion for about 5 minutes.
7. Add mushrooms, garlic and herbs and cook for about 5 minutes, stirring continuously.
8. Remove the pan of mushroom mixture from heat and set aside to cool for about 5 minutes.
9. Preheat your oven to 350°F.

10. Lightly grease a baking sheet.
11. In a bowl, add quinoa, mushroom mixture, cheese, egg, pecans, oats, and tamari and stir to combine well.
12. Make 8 equal-sized patties from the mixture.
13. Arrange the quinoa patties onto the prepared baking sheet in a single layer.
14. Bake for approximately 28–30 minutes or until top becomes golden brown.
15. Serve hot.

HERBED FOCACCIA

Preparation time: 15 minutes

Cooking time: 15 minutes

Total time: 30 minutes

Servings: 12

Nutritional Values

Calories 265, Total Fat 4.9 g, Saturated Fat 1.1 g, Cholesterol 3 mg

Sodium 60 mg, Total Carbs 46.9 g, Fiber 1.9 g, Sugar 0.6 g ,Protein 7.8 g

Ingredients

- 2¾ cups all-purpose flour
- 1 tablespoon active dry yeast
- 1 teaspoon white sugar
- 1 teaspoon dried thyme, crushed
- 1 teaspoon dried oregano, crushed
- ½ teaspoon dried basil, crushed
- 1 teaspoon garlic powder
- Salt, as needed
- Pinch of freshly ground black pepper
- 1 cup water
- 1 tablespoon vegetable oil
- 2 tablespoon olive oil
- 1 cup mozzarella cheese, grated
- 1 tablespoon Parmesan cheese, grated

How to Prepare

1. Place flour, yeast, sugar, dried herbs, garlic powder, salt, and black pepper and mix well.
2. Add water and vegetable oil and mix until a dough forms.
3. Place the dough onto a lightly floured surface and with your hands, knead until smooth and elastic.
4. Immediately place the dough into a lightly greased bowl and turn to coat well
5. With a damp cloth, cover the bowl and set aside in a warm place for 20 minutes.
6. Preheat your oven to 450°F.
7. Grease a baking sheet.
8. With your hands, punch the dough well.

9. Now place the dough onto the prepared baking sheet and with your hands, pat into a ½-inch thick rectangle.
10. Coat the top of dough with olive oil evenly and sprinkle with both cheeses.
11. Bake for approximately 15 minutes or until golden brown.
12. Remove the baking sheet from oven and place onto a wire rack to cool for about 5 minutes.
13. Now, turn the bread onto the wire rack.
14. With a knife, cut the bread into desired-sized pieces and serve warm.

CHAPTER 5:

SEAFOOD
RECIPES

LEMONY SALMON

Preparation time: 10 minutes

Cooking time: 8 minutes

Total time: 18 minutes

Servings: 4

Nutritional Values

Calories 157, Total Fat 7.3 g, Saturated Fat 1.1 g, Cholesterol 50 mg

Sodium 146 mg, Total Carbs 1.1 g, Fiber 0.4 g, Sugar 0.2 g, Protein 22.2 g

Ingredients

- ½ tablespoon grainy mustard
- 1 tablespoon fresh lemon juice
- 2 teaspoons fresh thyme leaves, chopped
- Salt and ground black pepper, as needed
- 2 (4-ounce) salmon fillets

How to Prepare

1. Preheat your oven to broiler.
2. Lightly grease a baking sheet.
3. Mix together the mustard, thyme, lemon juice, salt, and black pepper in a bowl.
4. Place the salmon fillets onto the prepared baking sheet and top with mustard mixture.
5. Broil for about 6–8 minutes.
6. Serve hot.

SPICED SALMON

Preparation time: 15 minutes

Cooking time: 15 minutes

Total time: 30 minutes

Servings: 6

Nutritional Values

Calories 287, Total Fat 16.5 g, Saturated Fat 5.2 g, Cholesterol 90 mg

Sodium 146 mg, Total Carbs 2.2 g, Fiber 0.6 g, Sugar 0.7 g, Protein 33.5 g

Ingredients

- 6 (6-ounce) salmon fillets
- Salt and ground black pepper, as needed
- 3–4 tablespoons unsalted butter
- 2–3 teaspoons garlic, minced
- 2–3 tablespoon fresh parsley, chopped
- 1 tablespoon onion powder
- 1 tablespoon paprika
- ½ teaspoon cayenne pepper
- 2 tablespoons fresh lemon juice

How to Prepare

1. Preheat your oven to 400°F.
2. Arrange a wire rack in the center of the oven.
3. Line a baking sheet with a foil piece.
4. Sprinkle each salmon fillet with salt and black pepper evenly. Set aside.
5. In a small saucepan, place butter, garlic, parsley, onion powder, paprika, and cayenne pepper over medium-low heat and cook for about 50-60 seconds, stirring continuously.
6. Remove the saucepan of butter mixture from heat and set aside for about 5 minutes.
7. After 5 minutes, in the pan, add the lemon juice and stir to combine.
8. Brush salmon with spice mixture evenly.
9. Bake for approximately 10–15 minutes or until desired doneness.
10. Serve hot.

PISTACHIO-CRUSTED SALMON

Preparation time: 15 minutes

Cooking time: 20 minutes

Total time: 35 minutes

Servings: 4

Nutritional Values

Calories 274, Total Fat 18.1 g, Saturated Fat 2.3 g, Cholesterol 50 mg

Sodium 305 mg, Total Carbs 6.1 g, Fiber 2.2 g, Sugar 1.5 g, Protein 25.6 g

Ingredients

- 1 cup pistachios
- 1 tablespoon fresh dill
- 2 tablespoons grated fresh lemon rind
- ½ teaspoon garlic powder
- Salt and ground black pepper, as needed
- 1 tablespoon olive oil
- 3 tablespoons Dijon mustard
- 4 (4-ounce) salmon fillets
- 4 teaspoons fresh lemon juice

How to Prepare

1. Preheat your oven to 350°F.
2. Line a baking sheet with parchment paper.
3. In a mini food processor, add pistachios and pulse until chopped roughly.
4. Add dill, lemon rind, garlic salt, black pepper, and oil and pulse until a crumbly mixture forms.
5. Place the salmon fillets onto the prepared baking sheet in a single layer, skin-side down.
6. Coat the top of each salmon fillet with Dijon mustard evenly.
7. Place the pistachio mixture over each fillet evenly and gently press into the surface of salmon.
8. Bake for approximately 16–20 minutes or until desired doneness of salmon.
9. Serve with the drizzling of lemon juice.

GLAZED SALMON

Preparation time: 10 minutes

Cooking time: 15 minutes

Total time: 25 minutes

Servings: 4

Nutritional Values

Calories 236, Total Fat 12.8 g, Saturated Fat 4.7 g, Cholesterol 65 mg

Sodium 131 mg, Total Carbs 9.2 g, Fiber 0.1 g, Sugar 8.7 g, Protein 22.2 g

Ingredients

- 2 tablespoons honey
- 2 tablespoons unsalted butter, melted
- 2 teaspoons fresh parsley, chopped
- 2 garlic cloves, minced
- 1/8 teaspoon paprika
- Salt and ground black pepper, as needed
- 4 (4-5-ounce) salmon fillets

How to Prepare

1. Preheat your oven to 400°F.
2. Line a baking sheet with a foil piece.
3. In a small bowl, mix together the honey, butter, parsley, garlic, paprika, salt, and black pepper and mix well.
4. Place the salmon fillets onto the prepared baking sheet in a single layer, skin-side down.
5. Place the honey mixture over the salmon fillets evenly.
6. Bake for approximately 8 minutes.
7. Remove the baking sheet from oven and baste the salmon fillets with pan sauce.
8. Bake for approximately 4–7 minutes or until desired doneness of salmon.

Salmon Parcel

Preparation time: 15 minutes

Cooking time: 20 minutes

Total time: 35 minutes

Servings: 6

Nutritional Values

Calories 224, Total Fat 14.3 g, Saturated Fat 2.2 g, Cholesterol 38 mg

Sodium 73 mg, Total Carbs 8.7 g, Fiber 2.5 g, Sugar 3.8 g, Protein 7.9 g

Ingredients

- 6 (3-ounce) fresh salmon fillets
- Salt and ground black pepper, as needed
- 3 bell peppers, seeded and thinly sliced (multi-colored)
- 12 cherry tomatoes, halved
- 1 small onion, sliced thinly
- ¼ cup fresh rosemary, chopped
- ¼ cup fresh dill, chopped
- ¼ cup extra-virgin olive oil
- 2 tablespoons fresh lemon juice

How to Prepare

1. Preheat your oven to 400°F.
2. Arrange 6 pieces of foil onto a smooth surface.
3. Place 1 salmon fillet on each foil piece and sprinkle with salt and black pepper.
4. In a bowl, mix together bell peppers, tomatoes, and onion.
5. Place veggie mixture over each fillet evenly.
6. Top with parsley and dill evenly.
7. Drizzle with oil and lemon juice.
8. Fold the foil around salmon mixture to seal it.
9. Arrange the foil packets onto a large baking sheet in a single layer.
10. Bake for approximately 20 minutes.
11. Serve hot.

SALMON & BEET BURGERS

Preparation time: 20 minutes

Cooking time: 20 minutes

Total time: 40 minutes

Servings: 6

Nutritional Values

Calories 158, Total Fat 5.2 g, Saturated Fat 0.6 g, Cholesterol 25 mg

Sodium 82 mg, Total Carbs 13.9 g, Fiber 2.5 g, Sugar 1.7 g, Protein 14.3 g

Ingredients

- 1 tablespoon beet powder
- 2 tablespoons ground flax seeds
- 5 tablespoon hot water
- 1 cooked large beet, peeled and chopped
- 2 (6-ounce) cans salmon
- ½ cup cooked quinoa
- ½ cup fresh kale, chopped
- ½ cup fresh parsley, chopped
- 2 garlic cloves, peeled
- Salt and ground black pepper, as needed

How to Prepare

1. Preheat your oven to 350°F.
2. Line a baking sheet with parchment paper.
3. In a bowl, add the flaxseeds and water and mix well.
4. In a food processor, add the beet and pulse until chopped.
5. Add the flax seeds mixture and remaining ingredients a chunky mixture is formed.
6. With your wet hands, make 6 equal-sized patties from the mixture.
7. Arrange the salmon patties onto the prepared baking sheet in a single layer.
8. Bake for approximately 15–20 minutes.
9. Serve hot.

LEMONY COD

Preparation time: 10 minutes

Cooking time: 18 minutes

Total time: 28 minutes

Servings: 2

Nutritional Values

Calories 196, Total Fat 7.4 g, Saturated Fat 3.7 g, Cholesterol 99 mg

Sodium 231 mg, Total Carbs 1.9 g, Fiber 0.4 g, Sugar 0 g, Protein 31.1 g

Ingredients

- 2 (6-ounce) cod fillets
- 1/8 teaspoon garlic powder
- Salt and ground black pepper, as needed
- 1 fresh dill sprig
- 2 lemon slices
- 1 tablespoon butter, melted

How to Prepare

1. Preheat your oven to 350°F.
2. Lightly grease a baking sheet.
3. Season the cod fillets with garlic powder, salt, and black pepper.
4. Arrange the cod fillets onto the prepared baking sheet and top with lemon slices and dill.
5. Drizzle the cod fillets with butter.
6. Bake for approximately 15–18 minutes or until desired doneness of cod fillets.
7. Serve hot.

COD WITH TOMATOES

Preparation time: 15 minutes

Cooking time: 24 minutes

Total time: 39 minutes

Servings: 4

Nutritional Values

Calories 221, Total Fat 10.8 g, Saturated Fat 4.2 g, Cholesterol 85 mg

Sodium 174 mg, Total Carbs 5.7 g, Fiber 1.5 g, Sugar 03.2 g, Protein 26.5 g

Ingredients

- 4 (5-ounce) cod fillets
- 1 tablespoon plus 1 teaspoon olive oil, divided
- 1 tablespoon fresh lemon juice
- 2 cups cherry tomatoes, halved
- 1 small onion, sliced
- 2 garlic cloves, minced
- ¼ teaspoon dried basil
- Salt and ground black pepper, as needed
- 2 tablespoons butter, melted

How to Prepare

1. Preheat your oven to 400°F.
2. Grease a large-rimmed baking sheet.
3. In a bowl, add cod, 1 teaspoon of olive oil, lemon juice, salt, and black pepper and mix well.
4. Refrigerate the cod fillets for about 10–15 minutes.
5. In a separate bowl, add tomatoes, onion, remaining olive oil, garlic, basil, salt, and black pepper and toss to coat.
6. Arrange the tomato mixture onto the prepared baking sheet.
7. Roast for about 10 minutes.
8. Remove the baking sheet from oven and arrange the cod fillets alongside the tomatoes.
9. Drizzle the cod fillets from melted butter.
10. Bake for approximately 11–14 minutes or until desired doneness of fish.
11. Serve hot.

TROUT WITH ASPARAGUS

Preparation time: 15 minutes

Cooking time: 15 minutes

Total time: 30 minutes

Servings: 3

Nutritional Values

Calories 446, Total Fat 27 g, Saturated Fat 4.3 g, Cholesterol 112 mg

Sodium 156 mg, Total Carbs 7.7 g, Fiber 3.4 g, Sugar 3 g, Protein 43.9 g

Ingredients

- 1 pound asparagus, trimmed
- 3 tablespoons olive oil
- 1 pound rainbow trout
- 5 garlic cloves, minced
- Salt and ground black pepper, as needed
- ½ lemon, sliced

How to Prepare

1. Preheat your oven to 400°F.
2. Line a baking sheet with parchment paper.
3. In a bowl, add the asparagus and half of oil and toss to coat well.
4. Arrange the trout onto the prepared baking sheet, skin-side down.
5. Coat the trout with the remaining olive oil evenly.
6. Now arrange the asparagus around the trout.
7. Sprinkle the trout and asparagus with garlic, salt, and black pepper.
8. Sprinkle the minced garlic on top of the trout fillet and asparagus.
9. Arrange the lemon slices on top of trout.
10. Bake for approximately 15 minutes.
11. Serve hot.

CHEESY TILAPIA

Preparation time: 10 minutes

Cooking time: 8 minutes

Total time: 18 minutes

Servings: 8

Nutritional Values

Calories 185, Total Fat 9.8 g, Saturated Fat 5 g, Cholesterol 76 mg

Sodium 163 mg, Total Carbs 1.5 g, Fiber 0 g, Sugar 0.4 g, Protein 23.3 g

Ingredients

- ½ cup Parmesan cheese, grated
- 3 tablespoons mayonnaise
- ¼ cup butter, softened
- 2 tablespoons fresh lemon juice
- ¼ teaspoon dried thyme, crushed
- 1/8 teaspoon celery salt
- 1/8 teaspoon onion powder
- Ground black pepper, as needed
- 2 pounds tilapia fillets

How to Prepare

1. Preheat your oven to broiler on High.
2. Grease a baking sheet.
3. In a bowl, add cheese, mayonnaise, butter, lemon juice, thyme, celery salt, onion powder, and black pepper and mix well.
4. Arrange the tilapia fillets onto the prepared baking sheet in a single layer.
5. Broil for about 2–3 minutes.
6. Remove from oven and top the fillets with cheese mixture evenly.
7. Broil for about 2 minutes more.

TILAPIA WITH CAPERS

Preparation time: 15 minutes

Cooking time: 15 minutes

Total time: 30 minutes

Servings: 4

Nutritional Values

Calories 150, Total Fat 5.8 g, Saturated Fat 3.3 g, Cholesterol 67 mg

Sodium 369 mg, Total Carbs 3.6 g, Fiber 0.7 g, Sugar 0.3 g, Protein 22 g

Ingredients

- 1½ teaspoons paprika
- 1½ teaspoons ground cumin
- Salt and ground black pepper, as needed
- 2 shallots, chopped finely
- 3 garlic cloves, minced
- 2 tablespoons fresh lemon juice
- 1½ tablespoons butter, melted
- 1 pound tilapia, cut into 8 pieces
- ¼ cup capers

How to Prepare

1. Preheat your oven to 375°F.
2. Line a rimmed baking sheet with a greased parchment paper.
3. In a small bowl, mix together the paprika, cumin, salt, and black pepper.
4. In another small bowl, add the butter, shallots, garlic, lemon juice, and butter and mix until well blended.
5. Season the tilapia fillets with the spice mixture evenly and cot with the butter mixture generously.
6. Arrange the tilapia fillets onto the prepared baking sheet and top with the capers.
7. Bake for approximately 10–15 minutes or until desired doneness of fish.
8. Serve hot.

HALIBUT WITH OLIVES & TOMATOES

Preparation time: 15 minutes

Cooking time: 40 minutes

Total time: 55 minutes

Servings: 4

Nutritional Values

Calories 365, Total Fat 20.7 g, Saturated Fat 2.9 g, Cholesterol 55 mg

Sodium 814 mg, Total Carbs 8.2g, Fiber 2.6 g, Sugar 2.5 g, Protein 37.2 g

Ingredients

- 1 onion, chopped
- 1 large tomato, chopped
- 1 (5-ounce) jar pitted kalamata olives
- ¼ cup capers
- ¼ cup olive oil
- 1 tablespoon fresh lemon juice
- Salt and ground black pepper, as needed
- 4 (6-ounce) halibut fillets
- 1 tablespoon Greek seasoning

How to Prepare

1. Preheat your oven to 350°F.
2. In a bowl, add the onion, tomato, olives, capers, oil, lemon juice, salt, and black pepper and mix well.
3. Season the halibut fillets with the Greek seasoning and arrange onto a large piece of foil.
4. Top the fillets with the tomato mixture.
5. Carefully fold all edges of foil to create a large packet.
6. Arrange the packet onto a baking sheet.
7. Bake for approximately 30–40 minutes.
8. Serve hot.

ROASTED SHRIMP

Preparation time: 15 minutes

Cooking time: 8 minutes

Total time: 23 minutes

Servings: 3

Nutritional Values

Calories 260, Total Fat 11.9 g, Saturated Fat 2.1 g, Cholesterol 318 mg

Sodium 419 mg, Total Carbs 2.3 g, Fiber 0 g, Sugar 0 g, Protein 34.4 g

Ingredients

- 1 pound shrimp, peeled and deveined
- 2 tablespoons olive oil
- Salt and ground black pepper, as needed

How to Prepare

1. Preheat your oven to 400°F.
2. Arrange a wire rack in the center position of oven.
3. Lightly grease a large baking sheet.
4. In a large bowl, add shrimp, oil, salt, and black pepper and toss to coat well.
5. Arrange the shrimp onto the prepared baking sheet in a single layer.
6. Roast for approximately 6–8 minutes or until opaque.
7. Serve hot.

SHRIMP PIZZA

Preparation time: 15 minutes

Cooking time: 10 minutes

Total time: 35 minutes

Servings: 6

Nutritional Values

Calories 252, Total Fat 9.6 g, Saturated Fat 2.7 g, Cholesterol 88 mg

Sodium 576 mg, Total Carbs 25.3 g, Fiber 1.3 g, Sugar 4.3 g, Protein 16.5 g

Ingredients

- 1 (12-inch) prepared pizza crust
- 1/3 cup prepared pesto sauce
- 2 cups mozzarella cheese, shredded and divided
- 8 ounces cooked shrimp, peeled and deveined
- ½ cup sun-dried tomatoes, chopped finely
- ¼ cup scallions, minced
- ¼ teaspoon red pepper flakes, crushed

How to Prepare

1. Preheat your oven to 450°F.
2. Arrange the pizza crust onto a baking sheet.
3. Spread the pesto sauce over crust evenly and sprinkle with half of the cheese.
4. Top with the shrimp, followed by the tomatoes, remaining cheese, scallion, and red pepper flakes.
5. Bake for approximately 10 minutes.
6. Remove the baking sheet of pizza from the oven and set aside for about 3–5 minutes before slicing.
7. Cut into desired-sized slices and serve.

GARLIC BUTTER LOBSTER TAILS

Preparation time: 10 minutes

Cooking time: 10 minutes

Total time: 20 minutes

Servings: 2

Nutritional Values

Calories 333, Total Fat 23.3 g, Saturated Fat 14.7 g, Cholesterol 131 mg

Sodium 550 mg, Total Carbs 6 g, Fiber 0.4 g, Sugar 0.5 g, Protein 25.8 g

Ingredients

- 4 tablespoons butter
- ¼ cup garlic, minced
- ¼ teaspoon paprika
- 2 tablespoons fresh lemon juice
- 2 lobster tails, top removed and deveined
- Salt and ground black pepper, as needed

How to Prepare

1. Preheat your oven to broiler on High.
2. Grease a baking sheet.
3. In a frying pan, add butter over medium heat and cook until melted.
4. Add the garlic and sauté for about 1 minute.
5. Remove the frying pan from heat and set aside.
6. Arrange the lobster tails onto the prepared baking sheet and sprinkle with paprika, salt, and black pepper.
7. Drizzle with half of the garlic butter.
8. Bake for approximately 10 minutes, drizzling with the remaining garlic butter occasionally.
9. Serve hot.

CHAPTER 6:

BEEF & PORK
RECIPES

GLAZED CORNED BEEF

Preparation time: 10 minutes

Cooking time: 1 hour 20 minutes

Total time: 1½ hours

Servings: 6

Nutritional Values

Calories 300, Total Fat 19.5 g, Saturated Fat 8.1 g, Cholesterol 95 mg

Sodium 852 mg, Total Carbs 9.7 g, Fiber 0.3 g, Sugar 8.8 g, Protein 20.8 g

Ingredients

- 2 pounds corned beef
- 5 tablespoons Dijon mustard
- 1 tablespoon whole grain mustard
- 1 tablespoon honey
- ¼ cup dark brown sugar

How to Prepare

1. Preheat your oven to 350°F.
2. Arrange the rack into the center position of oven.
3. Arrange a wire rack into a roasting pan.
4. Remove the beef from its package and discard the spice packet.
5. Place about 1-inch of water into the bottom of roasting pan.
6. Arrange the corned beef into the prepared roasting pan, fat-side up.
7. In a small bowl, combine the Dijon mustard, whole grain mustard, and honey.
8. Spread about 3 tablespoons of the mustard mixture on top of the beef evenly.
9. Sprinkle the top with 2 tablespoons of brown sugar.
10. With a piece of foil, cover the beef loosely.
11. Then cover the roasting pan with another piece of foil tightly.
12. Bake for approximately 75 minutes.
13. Remove the roasting pan of beef from oven and transfer the corned beef onto a foil-lined baking sheet.
14. Now set the oven to Broiler.
15. Top the corned beef with remaining mustard mixture, then sprinkle with remaining brown sugar.
16. Broil for about 3–5 minutes.
17. Remove the baking sheet from oven and place the beef onto a cutting board for about 10–15 minutes before slicing.
18. With a knife, cut the beef into desired-sized slices and serve.

GARLICKY PRIME RIB ROAST

Preparation time: 10 minutes

Cooking time: 1 hour 35 minutes

Total time: 1 hour 45 minutes

Servings: 16

Nutritional Values

Calories 693, Total Fat 52.4 g, Saturated Fat 20.5 g, Cholesterol 169 mg

Sodium 700 mg, Total Carbs 4 g, Fiber 0.1 g, Sugar 0 g, Protein 47.4 g

Ingredients

- 8–10 garlic cloves, minced
- 2 teaspoons dried thyme, crushed
- 2 tablespoons olive oil
- 1 teaspoon red pepper flakes, crushed
- Salt and ground black pepper, as needed
- 1 (10-pound) prime rib roast

How to Prepare

1. In a bowl, combine the garlic, thyme, oil, red pepper flakes, salt and black pepper.
2. Coat the rib roast with garlic mixture evenly.
3. In a large roasting pan, place rib roast, fatty-side up.
4. Set aside to marinate at room temperature for at least 1 hour.
5. Preheat your oven to 500°F.
6. Roast for approximately 20 minutes.
7. Now set the temperature of oven to 325°F.
8. Roast for 65–75 minutes.
9. Remove the roasting pan from oven and set aside for about 10–15 minutes before slicing.
10. With a sharp knife, cut the rib roast into desired-sized slices and serve.

CHEESE & CRUMB-CRUSTED RIB ROAST

Preparation time: 15 minutes

Cooking time: 2 hours

Total time: 2¼ hours

Servings: 8

Nutritional Values

Calories 797, Total Fat 52.8 g, Saturated Fat 22.1 g, Cholesterol 194 mg

Sodium 368 mg, Total Carbs 12.4 g, Fiber 2.2 g ,Sugar 0.9 g, Protein 64.8 g

Ingredients

- 4 pounds beef rib roast
- Salt and ground black pepper, as needed
- 2 tablespoons olive oil
- 2 tablespoons butter, melted
- 3 garlic cloves, minced
- ¼ cup Romano cheese, grated
- 1 cup plain breadcrumbs
- ½ cup fresh rosemary, minced

How to Prepare

1. Preheat your oven to 325°F.
2. Arrange a wire rack in a large roasting pan.
3. Season the rib roast with salt and black pepper.
4. In a bowl, combine the oil, butter, and garlic.
5. In a separate bowl, mix together cheese, breadcrumbs, and rosemary.
6. Brush the rib roast with oil mixture evenly and then coat with cheese mixture.
7. Arrange the rib roast into the prepared roasting pan.
8. Roast for approximately 2 hours or until desired doneness.
9. Remove the roasting pan from oven and set aside for about 10–15 minutes before slicing.
10. With a sharp knife, cut the rib roast into desired-sized slices and serve.

HERB-CRUSTED BEEF TENDERLOIN

Preparation time: 15 minutes

Cooking time: 50 minutes

Total time: 1 hour 5 minutes

Servings: 12

Nutritional Values

Calories 383, Total Fat 17.8 g, Saturated Fat 5.9 g, Cholesterol 140 mg

Sodium 244 mg, Total Carbs 8 g, Fiber 1 g, Sugar 0.8 g, Protein 45.3 g

Ingredients

- 1 (4-pound) beef tenderloin, trimmed and tied
- ¼ cup Dijon mustard
- 2 tablespoons mayonnaise
- 1 cup dry breadcrumbs
- 2 tablespoons olive oil
- 1 tablespoon fresh rosemary, minced
- 1 tablespoon fresh oregano, minced
- 1 tablespoon fresh thyme, minced
- ½ teaspoon garlic powder
- Salt and ground black pepper, as needed

How to Prepare

1. Place the beef tenderloin at room temperature for about 1 hour before cooking.
2. Preheat your oven to 375°F.
3. Place a wire rack onto a foil-lined baking sheet.
4. In a bowl, add mustard and mayonnaise and mix well.
5. In a separate bowl, add breadcrumbs, oil, herbs, garlic powder, salt, and black pepper and mix until blender well.
6. Brush the tenderloin with mustard mixture and then coat with breadcrumb mixture evenly.
7. Arrange the tenderloin into the prepared roasting pan.
8. Roast for approximately 45–50 minutes or until desired doneness.
9. Remove the roasting pan from oven and set the tenderloin aside for about 15–20 minutes before slicing.
10. With a knife, cut the cooked tenderloin into desired-sized slices and serve.

BEEF ROAST WITH VEGGIES

Preparation time: 15 minutes

Cooking time: 40 minutes

Total time: 55 minutes

Servings: 4

Nutritional Values

Calories 381, Total Fat 21 g, Saturated Fat 5.5 g, Cholesterol 104 mg

Sodium 225 mg, Total Carbs 12.9 g, Fiber 3.1 g, Sugar 2.7 g, Protein 34.8 g

Ingredients

- 3 tablespoons olive oil, divided
- 3 teaspoons fresh thyme, chopped
- 3 teaspoons garlic & herb seasoning, divided
- Salt and ground black pepper, as needed
- ½ pound baby potatoes
- 2 cups carrots, peeled and sliced
- 1 (1-pound) beef tenderloin

How to Prepare

1. Preheat your oven to 425°F.
2. Line a roasting pan with a foil piece.
3. In a bowl, mix together 1 tablespoon of olive oil, 1 teaspoon of thyme, 1 teaspoon of garlic & herb seasoning, salt, and black pepper.
4. Add the potatoes and carrots and toss to coat well.
5. In a second bowl, combine the remaining olive oil, thyme, garlic & herb seasoning, salt, and black pepper.
6. Rub the tenderloin with oil mixture generously.
7. Place the tenderloin into the prepared roasting pan and arrange the vegetables around it.
8. Roast for approximately 40 minutes, flipping the vegetables once after 20 minutes.
9. Remove the roasting pan of beef from oven and place onto a cutting board for about 10 minutes.
10. Cut the tenderloin into desired-sized slices and serve alongside the vegetables.

Sirloin Steak with Broccoli

Preparation time: 15 minutes

Cooking time: 14 minutes

Total time: 29 minutes

Servings: 4

Nutritional Values

Calories 352, Total Fat 11.6 g, Saturated Fat 3.3 g,Cholesterol 128 mg

Sodium 515 mg, Total Carbs 14.6 g, Fiber 2.6 g, Sugar 9.7 g, Protein 45.9 g

Ingredients

- ¼ cup sesame dressing
- 1 tablespoon low-sodium soy sauce
- 4 cups fresh broccoli florets
- 1 tablespoon brown sugar
- 1¼ pounds boneless beef sirloin steak, cut into 2-inch pieces
- 2 scallions (green part), chopped

How to Prepare

1. Preheat your oven to 450°F.
2. Grease a rimmed baking sheet.
3. In a bowl, mix together the dressing and 1 teaspoon of soy sauce.
4. Add the broccoli and toss to coat well.
5. In a separate bowl, add the steak pieces, remaining soy sauce, and brown sugar and toss to coat well.
6. Arrange the steak pieces and broccoli onto the prepared baking sheet in an even layer.
7. Bake for approximately 12–14 minutes or until desired doneness.
8. Serve hot with the garnishing of scallion greens.

Beef Wellington

Preparation time: 20 minutes

Cooking time: 40 minutes

Total time: 1 hour

Servings: 8

Nutritional Values

Calories 712, Total Fat 43.9 g, Saturated Fat 15 g, Cholesterol 200 mg

Sodium 308 mg, Total Carbs 29.9 g, Fiber 1.3 g, Sugar 1.1 g, Protein 47.2 g

Ingredients

- 2½ pounds beef tenderloin
- 4 tablespoons butter, softened and divided
- ½ cup fresh mushrooms, sliced
- 1 onion, chopped
- 2 ounces liver pate
- Salt and ground black pepper, as needed
- 1 (17½-ounce) package frozen puff pastry, thawed
- 1 egg yolk, beaten

How to Prepare

1. Preheat your oven to 450°F.
2. Rub the beef tenderloin with 2 tablespoons of butter.
3. Arrange the beef tenderloin onto a baking sheet and bake for approximately 10–15 minutes or until browned.
4. Remove the beef tenderloin from oven and set aside to cool completely.
5. Melt 2 tablespoons of butter in a wok over medium heat and sauté the mushrooms and onion for about 5 minutes.
6. Remove the mushroom mixture from heat and set aside to cool.
7. In a bowl, add remaining butter, liver pate, salt, and black pepper and mix well.
8. Spread pate mixture over beef and top with mushroom mixture.
9. With clean hands, roll out the pastry dough.
10. Place the beef in the center of rolled dough.
11. Fold up, and seal all the edges.
12. Arrange the beef onto a rimmed baking sheet.
13. With a knife, cut a few slits in the top of the dough, and brush with beaten egg yolk.
14. Bake for approximately 10 minutes.
15. Now set the temperature of oven to 425°F.
16. Bake for approximately 10–15 minutes or until pastry is golden brown.
17. Serve warm.

SIMPLE PORK BELLY

Preparation time: 10 minutes

Cooking time: 2½ hours

Total time: 2 hours 40 minutes

Servings: 6

Nutritional Values

Calories 467, Total Fat 42 g, Saturated Fat 13.1 g, Cholesterol 80 mg

Sodium 650 mg, Total Carbs 0 g, Fiber 0 g, Sugar 0 g, Protein 23.1 g

Ingredients

- 2 pounds pork belly with skin.
- Salt and ground black pepper, as needed
- 2 tablespoons olive oil

How to Prepare

1. Preheat your oven to 350°F.
2. Arrange a wire rack into a roasting pan.
3. With a knife, make many cuts across the skin of the pork belly, about ¼-inch apart.
4. Season the pork belly with salt and black pepper and then drizzle with oil.
5. Arrange the pork belly into the prepared roasting pan, skin-side up.
6. Roast for approximately 2–2½ hours.
7. Remove the roasting pan of pork belly from oven and place onto a cutting board for about 10–15 minutes.
8. With a sharp knife, cut into desired-sized slices and serve.

GARLICKY PORK SHOULDER

Preparation time: 10 minutes

Cooking time: 6 hours

Total time: 6 hours 10 minutes

Servings: 12

Nutritional Values

Calories 450, Total Fat 32.6 g, Saturated Fat 12 g, Cholesterol 136 mg

Sodium 104 mg, Total Carbs 1.7 g, Fiber 0.6 g, Sugar 0.1 g, Protein 35.4 g

Ingredients

- 1 head garlic, peeled and crushed
- ¼ cup fresh rosemary, minced
- 2 tablespoons fresh lemon juice
- 2 tablespoons balsamic vinegar
- 1 (4-pound) pork shoulder

How to Prepare

1. In a bowl, add garlic, rosemary, lemon juice, and vinegar and mix well.
2. In a large roasting pan, place pork shoulder and coat with marinade generously.
3. Cover with a large plastic wrap and refrigerate to marinate for at least 1–2 hours.
4. Remove the roasting pan from refrigerator.
5. Remove the plastic wrap from roasting pan and se aside at room temperature for 1 hour.
6. Preheat your oven to 275°F.
7. Roast for approximately 6 hours.
8. Remove the roasting pan of pork shoulder from oven and place onto a cutting board for about 15–20 minutes.
9. With a sharp knife, cut into desired-sized slices and serve.

CRUSTED PORK TENDERLOIN

Preparation time: 15 minutes

Cooking time: 22 minutes

Total time: 37 minutes

Servings: 5

Nutritional Values

Calories 344, Total Fat 13.1 g, Saturated Fat 2.8 g, Cholesterol 110 mg

Sodium 184 mg, Total Carbs 15.7 g, Fiber 0.9 g, Sugar 12.5 g, Protein 41.1 g

Ingredients

- 1/3 cup pistachios, toasted
- 2 garlic cloves, peeled
- 1 pound pork tenderloin, trimmed
- Salt and ground black pepper, as needed
- 1 tablespoon extra-virgin olive oil
- 3 tablespoons orange marmalade

How to Prepare

1. Preheat your oven to 450°F.
2. Arrange a wire rack in the center position of oven.
3. Grease a baking sheet.
4. In a mini food processor, add pistachios and garlic and pulse until finely chopped.
5. Sprinkle the pork with salt and black pepper.
6. In a skillet, heat oil over medium-high heat and cook the pork for about 4–6 minutes or until browned.
7. Remove the skillet of pork from heat and transfer the pork onto the prepared baking sheet.
8. Coat the top of pork with orange marmalade, followed by pistachio mixture.
9. Bake for approximately 12–16 minutes.
10. Remove the baking sheet from oven and place the tenderloin onto a cutting board for about 10 minutes.
11. With a sharp knife, cut into desired-sized slices and serve.

BACON-WRAPPED PORK TENDERLOIN

Preparation time: 10 minutes

Cooking time: 23 minutes

Total time: 33 minutes

Servings: 3

Nutritional Values

Calories 631, Total Fat 37.3 g, Saturated Fat 12.3 g, Cholesterol 195 mg

Sodium 2,000 mg, Total Carbs 1.1 g, Fiber 0 g, Sugar 0 g, Protein 68 g

Ingredients

- 1 pound pork tenderloin
- 1 tablespoon Southwest seasoning
- 8 bacon slices

How to Prepare

1. Preheat your oven to 400°F.
2. Line a baking sheet with a foil piece.
3. Season the pork with seasoning evenly.
4. Wrap the pork tenderloin with bacon slices and then secure with toothpicks.
5. Place pork tenderloin onto the prepared baking sheet.
6. Bake for approximately 18–20 minutes.
7. Now set the oven to broiler.
8. Broil for about 2–3 minutes.
9. Remove the baking sheet from oven and place the tenderloin onto a cutting board for about 10 minutes.
10. Cut the tenderloin into desired-sized slices and serve alongside the vegetables.

GARLICKY PORK LOIN ROAST

Preparation time: 10 minutes

Cooking time: 1 hour

Total time: 1 hour 10 minutes

Servings: 6

Nutritional Values

Calories 293, Total Fat 13.8 g, Saturated Fat 3.1 g, Cholesterol 110 mg

Sodium 114 mg, Total Carbs 1 g, Fiber 0.3 g, Sugar 0 g, Protein 39.7 g

Ingredients

- 4 garlic cloves, chopped
- 1 tablespoon dried rosemary, crushed
- Salt and ground black pepper, as needed
- 2 pounds boneless pork loin roast
- ¼ cup olive oil

How to Prepare

1. Preheat your oven to 350°F.
2. Lightly grease a roasting pan.
3. In a small bowl, add garlic, rosemary, salt, and black pepper and with the back of a spoon, crush until a paste forms.
4. With a knife, pierce the pork loin at many places.
5. Press half of the rosemary mixture into the cuts.
6. Add oil in the bowl with the remaining rosemary mixture and stir to combine.
7. Rub the pork with oil mixture generously.
8. Place the pork loin into the prepared roasting pan.
9. Roast for approximately 1 hour, flipping and coating with the pan juices occasionally.
10. Remove the roasting pan of pork from oven and place onto a cutting board for about 10 minutes.
11. With a sharp knife, cut into desired-sized slices and serve.

GLAZED PORK RIBS

Preparation time: 15 minutes

Cooking time: 2 hours 34 minutes

Total time: 2 hours 49 minutes

Servings: 4

Nutritional Values

Calories 511, Total Fat 26.5 g, Saturated Fat 10.1 g, Cholesterol 91 mg

Sodium 950 mg, Total Carbs 26.5 g, Fiber 0.5 g, Sugar 21.1 g, Protein 40.7 g

Ingredients

- 2–3 tablespoons granulated honey
- ½ tablespoon garlic powder
- 2 pounds pork ribs, membrane removed
- Salt and ground black pepper, as needed
- ¾ teaspoon liquid smoke
- ¾ cup BBQ sauce

How to Prepare

1. Preheat your oven to 300°F.
2. Line a baking sheet with 2 heavy-duty foil pieces.
3. In a bowl, add the honey and garlic powder and mix well.
4. Sprinkle the ribs with salt and black pepper evenly and then coat with the liquid smoke.
5. Now, rub the ribs with honey mixture evenly.
6. Arrange ribs onto the prepared baking sheet, meaty-side down.
7. Arrange two layers of foil on top of ribs and then roll and crimp edges tightly.
8. Bake for approximately 2–2½ hours or until desired doneness.
9. Remove the baking sheet from oven and place the ribs onto a cutting board.
10. Now, set the oven to broiler.
11. With a knife, cut the ribs into serving-sized portions and evenly coat with the BBQ sauce.
12. Arrange the ribs onto another baking sheet, bony-side up.
13. Broil for about 1–2 minutes per side.
14. Remove from the oven and serve hot.

HERBED PORK MEATBALLS

Preparation time: 15 minutes

Cooking time: 35 minutes

Total time: 50 minutes

Servings: 6

Nutritional Values

Calories 257, Total Fat 17.9 g, Saturated Fat 0.3 g, Cholesterol 27 mg

Sodium 483 mg, Total Carbs 3.3 g, Fiber 0.6 g, Sugar 0.9 g, Protein 21 g

Ingredients

- 1 lemongrass stalk, peeled and chopped
- 1 (1½-inch) piece fresh ginger, chopped
- 3 garlic cloves, chopped
- 1 cup fresh cilantro leaves, chopped
- ½ cup fresh basil leaves, chopped
- 2 tablespoons plus 1 teaspoon fish sauce
- 2 tablespoons water
- 2 tablespoons fresh lime juice
- 1½ pounds lean ground pork
- 1 carrot, peeled and grated
- 1 egg, beaten

How to Prepare

1. Preheat your oven to 375°F.
2. Grease a rimmed baking sheet.
3. **For meatballs:** In a food processor, add lemongrass, ginger, garlic, fresh herbs, fish sauce, water, and lime juice and pulse until chopped finely.
4. Transfer the mixture into a bowl with remaining ingredients and mix until well blended.
5. Make about 1-inch balls from the mixture.
6. Place the pork meatballs onto the prepared baking sheet and arrange in a single layer.
7. Bake for approximately 30–35 minutes.
8. Serve hot.

GLAZED HAM

Preparation time: 15 minutes

Cooking time: 1¼ hours

Total time: 1½ hours

Servings: 15

Nutritional Values

Calories 476, Total Fat 21.5 g, Saturated Fat 9.7 g, Cholesterol 108 mg

Sodium 1,652 mg, Total Carbs 48 g, Fiber 2.6 g, Sugar 38.5 g, Protein 25.4 g

Ingredients

- 1 (5-pound) ready-to-eat ham
- ¼ cup whole cloves
- 2 cups honey
- ¼ cup dark corn syrup
- 2/3 cup butter

How to Prepare

1. Preheat your oven to 325°F.
2. Line a large roasting pan with a piece of foil.
3. With a sharp knife, make small slits in the whole ham.
4. Insert the cloves inside the slits.
5. **For glaze:** In the top half of a double boiler, heat the honey, corn syrup, and butter until well blended.
6. Remove the glaze from heat and set aside.
7. Arrange the ham into the prepared roasting pan.
8. Roast for approximately 70 minutes, coating the ham with glaze after every 10–15 minutes.
9. Now, set the oven to broiler and broil for about 5 minutes.
10. Remove the roasting pan from oven and set aside for about 10 minutes.
11. With a sharp knife, cut the ham into desired-sized slices and serve.

CHEESE MEATLOAF

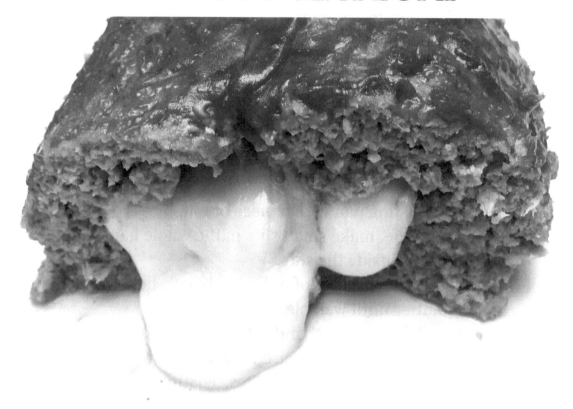

Preparation time: 20 minutes

Cooking time: 1 hour 17 minutes

Total time: 1 hour 37 minutes

Servings: 6

Nutritional Values

Calories 370, Total Fat 19.4 g, Saturated Fat 7.1 g, Cholesterol 135 mg

Sodium 852 mg, Total Carbs 6.5 g, Fiber 0.7 g, Sugar 3.6 g, Protein 37.8 g

Ingredients

- 6 bacon strips
- ½ medium onion, diced
- 1 carrot, peeled and chopped finely
- 1 garlic clove, minced
- 1 pound ground beef
- ¼ cup panko breadcrumbs
- 1 large egg
- 2 tablespoons tomato sauce
- 2 tablespoons Worcestershire sauce
- 1 tablespoon dried parsley
- 1 teaspoon garlic powder
- 1 teaspoon sea salt
- ½ teaspoon ground black pepper
- 2 mozzarella string cheese sticks
- 2 tablespoons ketchup

How to Prepare

1. Preheat your oven to 375°F.
2. Line a baking sheet with a heavy-duty foil piece.
3. Heat a nonstick skillet over medium and cook the bacon for about 7-10 minutes.
4. With a slotted spoon, transfer the bacon onto a paper towel-lined plate to drain.
5. Reserve the bacon grease inside the skillet.
6. After cooling, crumble the bacon.
7. In the bacon grease, add the carrots and onions over medium heat and sauté for about 5 minutes.
8. Add the garlic and sauté for about 2 minutes.

9. Remove the skillet from heat and with a slotted spoon, transfer the onion mixture into a bowl.
10. In a large bowl, add the beef, crumbled bacon, onion mixture, breadcrumbs, egg, tomato sauce, Worcestershire sauce, parsley, garlic powder, salt, and black pepper and mix until well blended.
11. Place the beef mixture onto the prepared baking sheet and pat into ½-inch thickness.
12. Place the string cheese sticks in the middle of the meat mixture and then shape into a meatloaf
13. Place the ketchup on top of the loaf and spread evenly.
14. Bake for approximately 50–60 minutes.
15. Remove the baking sheet from oven and set aside to cool for about 10 minutes before slicing.
16. Cut into desired-sized slices and serve.

186

CHAPTER 7:

SNACK

RECIPES

CANDIED PECANS

Preparation time: 10 minutes

Cooking time: 7 minutes

Total time: 17 minutes

Servings: 12

Nutritional Values

Calories 259, Total Fat 24.2 g, Saturated Fat 3.5 g, Cholesterol 5 mg

Sodium 172 mg, Total Carbs 10.5 g, Fiber 3.4 g, Sugar 7 g, Protein 3.4 g

Ingredients

- 3 cups raw pecans
- 2 tablespoons salted butter
- ½ cup light brown sugar
- ¼ cup water
- ½ teaspoon ground cinnamon
- 1 teaspoon sea salt
- 1 teaspoon vanilla extract

How to Prepare

1. Preheat your oven to 350°F.
2. Line a baking sheet with parchment paper.
3. In a non-stick wok, melt butter over medium heat and cook the pecans for about 3 minutes, stirring continuously.
4. Add in the brown sugar, and cook for about 2 minutes, stirring continuously.
5. Stir in the water, cinnamon, and salt and cook for about 1–2 minutes, stirring continuously.
6. Add in the vanilla extract and remove the pan of pecans from heat.
7. Transfer the pecans onto the prepared baking sheet and spread in an even layer.
8. Bake for approximately 5–7 minutes or until pecans become lightly crisp.
9. Remove the baking sheet from oven and set aside to cool completely before serving.

Sweet & Sour Chicken Wings

Preparation time: 15 minutes

Cooking time: 50 minutes

Total time: 1 hour 5 minutes

Servings: 4

Nutritional Values

Calories 408, Total Fat 14.8 g, Saturated Fat 3.9 g, Cholesterol 152 mg

Sodium 1,036 mg, Total Carbs 13.5 g, Fiber 1.3 g, Sugar 8 g, Protein 51.6 g

Ingredients

<u>Chicken Wings</u>
- 1½ pounds chicken wings
- 4 garlic cloves, minced
- 1 tablespoon fresh ginger, minced
- ¼ cup tomato sauce
- ¼ cup soy sauce
- 2 tablespoons oyster sauce
- 2 tablespoons hoisin sauce
- 2 tablespoons sambal oelek
- 2 tablespoons red wine
- 2 tablespoons fresh lemon juice
- ½ teaspoon sesame oil
- 2 tablespoons brown sugar
- ½ teaspoon five-spice powder

<u>Topping</u>
- 2 tablespoons scallion, chopped
- 1 tablespoon sesame seeds

How to Prepare

1. **For chicken wings:** In a bowl, add all ingredients and mix until well blended and sugar is dissolved.
2. Cover the bowl of wings and set aside at room temperature for about 30 minutes.
3. Preheat your oven to 350°F.
4. Lightly grease a baking sheet.
5. Transfer the chicken wings onto the prepared baking sheet and spread in an even layer.
6. Bake for approximately 45–50 minutes.
7. Serve hot with the garnishing of scallions and sesame seeds.

CHEESY ZUCCHINI CHIPS

Preparation time: 15 minutes

Cooking time: 20 minutes

Total time: 35 minutes

Servings: 6

Nutritional Values

Calories 50, Total Fat 3.4 g, Saturated Fat 2.1 g, Cholesterol 10 mg

Sodium 145 mg, Total Carbs 1.6 g, Fiber 0.4 g, Sugar 0.7 g, Protein 3.7 g

Ingredients

- 2 small zucchinis, sliced into small rounds
- Salt and ground black pepper, as needed
- 1/8 teaspoon ground turmeric
- 1/3 cup Parmesan cheese, shredded
- 1/3 cup cheddar cheese, shredded

How to Prepare

1. Preheat your oven to 425°F.
2. Grease a baking sheet.
3. Season the zucchini rounds with turmeric, salt, and black pepper.
4. Arrange the zucchini rounds onto the prepared baking sheet and sprinkle evenly with cheeses.
5. Bake for approximately 20 minutes or until the cheese turns golden brown.
6. Serve warm.

Cheesy Tomato Slices

Preparation time: 15 minutes

Cooking time: 15 minutes

Total time: 30 minutes

Servings: 10

Nutritional Values

Calories 110, Total Fat 57.4 g, Saturated Fat 2.6 g, Cholesterol 16 mg

Sodium 227 mg, Total Carbs 6.7 g, Fiber 1.1 g, Sugar 2.7 g, Protein 5 g

Ingredients

- ½ cup mayonnaise
- ½ cup ricotta cheese, shredded
- ½ cup part-skim mozzarella cheese, shredded
- ½ cup Parmesan and Romano cheese blend, grated
- 1 teaspoon garlic, minced
- 1 tablespoon dried oregano, crushed
- Salt, to taste
- 4 large tomatoes, cut each one in 5 slices

How to Prepare

1. Preheat your oven to broiler on High.
2. Arrange an oven rack about 3-inch from the heating element.
3. In a bowl, add the mayonnaise, cheeses, garlic, oregano, and salt and mix until well blended.
4. Spread the cheese mixture over each tomato slice evenly.
5. Arrange the tomato slices onto a baking sheet in a single layer.
6. Broil for approximately 3–5 minutes or until top becomes golden brown.
7. Remove from the oven and transfer the tomato slices onto a platter.
8. Set aside to cool slightly.
9. Serve warm.

SWEET POTATO CROQUETTES

Preparation time: 15 minutes

Cooking time: 30 minutes

Total time: 45 minutes

Servings: 4

Nutritional Values

Calories 362, Total Fat 21.1 g, Saturated Fat 7.5 g, Cholesterol 82 mg

Sodium 124 mg, Total Carbs 36.3 g, Fiber 8 g, Sugar 10.9 g, Protein 10.8 g

Ingredients

- 3 cups cooked sweet potato, mashed
- 2 tablespoons coconut oil, melted
- Pinch of salt
- 2 eggs, beaten
- 1 cup almond meal

How to Prepare

1. Preheat your oven to 400°F.
2. Line a baking sheet with parchment paper.
3. In a bowl, add mashed sweet potatoes, coconut oil, and salt and mix well.
4. Place the beaten eggs and almond meal in 2 different bowls, respectively.
5. With 1 heaping tablespoon of the sweet potato mixture, make balls.
6. With your hands, press each ball into an oblong-shaped patty.
7. Dip each croquette into eggs and then coat with flour mixture.
8. Arrange the croquettes onto the prepared baking sheet in a single layer.
9. Bake for approximately 25–30 minutes or until golden brown.
10. Serve warm.

CHEDDAR CRISPS

Preparation time: 15 minutes

Cooking time: 5 minutes

Total time: 20 minutes

Servings: 4

Nutritional Values

Calories 107, Total Fat 18.5 g, Saturated Fat 5.3 g, Cholesterol 26 mg

Sodium 218 mg, Total Carbs 0.6 g, Fiber 0.1 g, Sugar 0.1 g, Protein 7.2 g

Ingredients

- ¾ cup sharp cheddar cheese, shredded finely
- 4 tablespoons Parmesan cheese, shredded
- ¼ teaspoon ground cumin
- ¼ teaspoon red chili powder
- 1/8 teaspoon cayenne pepper

How to Prepare

1. Preheat your oven to 400°F.
2. Lightly grease a baking sheet.
3. Place cheeses, cumin, chili powder, and cayenne pepper in a bowl and mix well.
4. Spoon the cheese mixture onto the prepared baking sheet about 1 inch apart.
5. Bake for approximately 5 minutes or until cheddar crisps become golden brown.
6. Serve warm.

CHEESE BISCUITS

Preparation time: 15 minutes

Cooking time: 15 minutes

Total time: 30 minutes

Servings: 6

Nutritional Values

Calories 399, Total Fat 23.4 g, Saturated Fat 14.3 g, Cholesterol 94 mg

Sodium 447 mg, Total Carbs 36.8 g, Fiber 1.2 g, Sugar 3.6 g, Protein 11.1 g

Ingredients

- 2 cups all-purpose flour
- 1 cup cheddar cheese, shredded
- 1 tablespoon baking powder
- 1 tablespoon sugar
- ½ teaspoon garlic powder
- ½ teaspoon salt
- 1 large egg
- 2/3 cup milk
- 1/3 cup butter
- 2 tablespoons unsalted butter, melted

How to Prepare

1. Preheat your oven to 400°F.
2. Grease a baking sheet.
3. In a bowl, add flour, cheddar cheese, baking powder, garlic powder, and salt and mix well.
4. In a second bowl, add egg, milk and 1/3 cup of butter and beat until well blended.
5. In the bowl of milk mixture, add the flour mixture and stir until just blended.
6. With a spoon, place dough onto the prepared baking sheet about 2 inches apart.
7. Bake for approximately 10 minutes.
8. Remove the baking sheet of biscuits from oven and brush each biscuit with melted butter.
9. Bake for approximately 5 minutes or until top of biscuits become golden brown.
10. Serve warm.

CAULIFLOWER BREADSTICKS

Preparation time: 15 minutes

Cooking time: 20 minutes

Total time: 35 minutes

Servings: 4

Nutritional Values

Calories 202, Total Fat 15.4 g, Saturated Fat 9.4 g, Cholesterol 91 mg

Sodium 335 mg, Total Carbs 3.3 g, Fiber 1.3 g, Sugar 1.6 g, Protein 13.1 g

Ingredients

- 2 cups cauliflower, riced
- 1½ cups cheddar cheese, shredded
- 1 large egg, beaten
- ¼ teaspoon dried Italian seasoning
- Salt and ground black pepper, as needed

How to Prepare

1. Preheat your oven to 475°F.
2. Lightly grease a baking sheet.
3. Add all ingredients in a bowl and with a wooden spoon, mix until well blended.
4. Place the cauliflower mixture onto the prepared baking sheet and spread in an even layer.
5. Bake for approximately 20 minutes.
6. Remove the baking sheet from oven and set aside to cool slightly.
7. Cut the cauliflower mixture into desired-sized breadsticks and serve.

RAISIN CRACKERS

Preparation time: 15 minutes

Cooking time: 12 minutes

Total time: 27 minutes

Servings: 25

Nutritional Values

Calories 68, Total Fat 5.6 g, Saturated Fat 0.5 g, Cholesterol 7 mg

Sodium 49 mg, Total Carbs 2.2 g, Fiber 1 g, Sugar 0.8 g, Protein 0.3 g

Ingredients

- 2 cups blanched almond flour
- 2 tablespoons raisins, chopped finely
- ½ teaspoon fresh rosemary, minced
- ½ teaspoon fresh thyme, minced
- ½ teaspoon salt
- 1 large egg
- 1 tablespoon olive oil
- 1 teaspoon water

How to Prepare

1. Preheat your oven to 350°F.
2. Line 2 cookie sheets with parchment paper.
3. In a large bowl, mix together flour, raisins, herbs, and salt.
4. In a second bowl, add remaining ingredients and beat until well blended.
5. Add egg mixture into the bowl of flour mixture and mix until a ball-like dough forms.
6. Arrange the dough onto a lightly floured surface and with a lightly floured rolling pin, roll the dough into 1/8-inch thickness.
7. With a knife, cut the dough into desired-shaped crackers.
8. Arrange the crackers onto the prepared cookie sheets in a single layer.
9. Bake for approximately 12 minutes or until top of cookies become golden.
10. Remove the cookie sheets from oven and let the crackers cool completely before serving.

BANANA & COCONUT COOKIES

Preparation time: 10 minutes

Cooking time: 25 minutes

Total time: 35 minutes

Servings: 6

Nutritional Values

Calories 56, Total Fat 3.4 g, Saturated Fat 3 g, Cholesterol 0 mg

Sodium 2 mg, Total Carbs 6.7 g, Fiber 1.5 g, Sugar 3.4 g, Protein 0.6 g

Ingredients

- 1 large banana, peeled and sliced
- ¾ cup unsweetened coconut, shredded
- ¼ teaspoon vanilla extract

How to Prepare

1. Preheat your oven to 350°F.
2. Line a cookie sheet with a greased parchment paper.
3. In a large food processor, add all ingredients and pulse until well blended.
4. With a spoon, place the dough onto the prepared cookie sheet.
5. With your hands, flatten each cookie slightly.
6. Bake for approximately 24-25 minutes or until top of cookies become golden.
7. Remove the cookie sheet from oven and place onto a wire rack to cool for about 5 minutes.
8. Now invert the cookies onto the wire rack to cool completely before serving.

LEMON COOKIES

Preparation time: 10 minutes

Cooking time: 12 minutes

Total time: 22 minutes

Servings: 6

Nutritional Values

Calories 287, Total Fat 21.2 g, Saturated Fat 4.2 g, Cholesterol 0 mg

Sodium 48 mg, Total Carbs 20.8 g, Fiber 0.9 g, Sugar 7.9 g, Protein 7.6 g

Ingredients

- ¼ cup pure maple syrup
- 1 cup cashew butter
- 1 teaspoon fresh lemon zest, grated finely
- 2 tablespoons fresh lemon juice
- Pinch of sea salt

How to Prepare

1. Preheat your oven to 350°F.
2. Line a cookie sheet with parchment paper.
3. In a clean food processor, add all ingredients and pulse until smooth.
4. With a tablespoon, place the mixture onto prepared cookie sheet in a single layer.
5. Bake for approximately 12 minutes or until top of cookies become golden.
6. Remove the cookie sheet of cookies from oven and place onto a wire rack to cool for about 5 minutes.
7. Now invert the cookies onto the wire rack to cool completely before serving.

CHICKEN POPCORN

Preparation time: 15 minutes

Cooking time: 25 minutes

Total time: 40 minutes

Servings: 3

Nutritional Values

Calories 403, Total Fat 34.3 g, Saturated Fat 23.4 g, Cholesterol 64 mg

Sodium 332 mg, Total Carbs 10.2 g, Fiber 3.9 g, Sugar 4.7 g, Protein 15.8 g

Ingredients

- 8 ounces boneless chicken thighs, cut into bite-sized pieces
- 7 ounces coconut milk
- 1 teaspoon ground turmeric
- Salt and ground black pepper, as needed
- 2 tablespoons coconut flour
- 3 tablespoons desiccated coconut
- 1 tablespoon coconut oil, melted

How to Prepare

1. In a large bowl, mix together chicken, coconut milk, turmeric, salt, and black pepper.
2. Refrigerate (covered) overnight.
3. Preheat your oven to 390°F.
4. Lightly greases a baking sheet.
5. In a shallow dish, add coconut flour and desiccated coconut and mix well.
6. Coat each chicken piece with coconut mixture evenly.
7. Arrange the chicken piece onto the prepared baking sheet and drizzle with oil evenly.
8. Bake for approximately 20–25 minutes.
9. Serve warm.

CHICKEN NUGGETS

Preparation time: 15 minutes

Cooking time: 15 minutes

Total time: 30 minutes

Servings: 4

Nutritional Values

Calories 476, Total Fat 16.3 g, Saturated Fat 4.4 g, Cholesterol 103 mg

Sodium 274 mg, Total Carbs 13.9 g, Fiber 0.5 g, Sugar 0.1 g, Protein 26.3 g

Ingredients

- 2 teaspoons olive oil
- 1/3 cup Italian seasoned breadcrumbs
- 2 tablespoons panko breadcrumbs
- 2 tablespoons Parmesan cheese, grated
- 16 ounces skinless, boneless chicken breast halves, cut into 1½-inch pieces
- Salt and ground black pepper, as needed
- Olive oil cooking spray

How to Prepare

1. Preheat your oven to 425°F.
2. Grease a large baking sheet.
3. In a shallow bowl, place the oil.
4. In another shallow bowl, mix together the seasoned breadcrumbs, panko, and Parmesan cheese.
5. Season the chicken pieces with salt and black pepper.
6. Dip the chicken pieces in oil and then coat with panko mixture.
7. Arrange the coated chicken pieces onto the prepared baking sheet in a single layer.
8. Lightly spray the top of chicken pieces with olive oil spray.
9. Bake for approximately 8–10 minutes.
10. Carefully flip the chicken pieces and bake for approximately 4–5 minutes.
11. Serve warm.

COD STICKS

Preparation time: 15 minutes

Cooking time: 12 minutes

Total time: 27 minutes

Servings: 4

Nutritional Values

Calories 144, Total Fat 2.2 g, Saturated Fat 0.4 g, Cholesterol 88 mg

Sodium 110 mg, Total Carbs 12.3 g, Fiber 0.6 g, Sugar 0.2 g, Protein 18.4 g

Ingredients

- 1 large egg
- ½ cup all-purpose flour
- ½ teaspoons dried thyme, crushed
- ½ teaspoon dried oregano, crushed
- ¼ teaspoon paprika
- Salt and ground black pepper, as needed
- 2 (6-ounce) cod fillets, sliced thinly

How to Prepare

1. Preheat your oven to 350°F.
2. Lightly grease a large baking sheet.
3. In a shallow dish, crack the egg and beat lightly.
4. In a second shallow dish, add flour, herbs, paprika, salt, and black pepper and mix well.
5. Dip each fish stick in the beaten egg and then coat with flour mixture completely.
6. Arrange the cod sticks onto the prepared baking sheet in a single layer.
7. Bake for approximately 10–12 minutes, flipping once halfway through.
8. Serve warm.

BACON-WRAPPED SCALLOPS

Preparation time: 15 minutes

Cooking time: 15 minutes

Total time: 30 minutes

Servings: 8

Nutritional Values

Calories 433, Total Fat 24.5 g, Saturated Fat 7.6 g, Cholesterol 100 mg

Sodium 1,352 mg, Total Carbs 10.3 g, Fiber 0 g, Sugar 6.1 g, Protein 40.3 g

Ingredients

- 2 pounds large sea scallops
- 1 pound bacon slices, halved crosswise
- ¼ cup maple syrup
- 2 tablespoons low-sodium soy sauce
- Ground black pepper, as needed

How to Prepare

1. Preheat your oven to broiler on High.
2. Lightly grease a large baking sheet.
3. Wrap each scallop with 1 bacon slice and secure with a toothpick.
4. Arrange the scallops onto the prepared baking sheet in a single layer.
5. In a mixing bowl, mix together the maple syrup, soy sauce and black pepper.
6. Brush the top of each scallop with half of the maple mixture.
7. Broil for about 10–15 minutes or until bacon is crisp and scallops are cooked through, coating with remaining maple mixture once halfway through.
8. Serve warm.

218

CHAPTER 8:

SWEETS
RECIPES

GLAZED FIGS

Preparation time: 10 minutes

Cooking time: 20 minutes

Total time: 30 minutes

Servings: 7

Nutritional Values

Calories 109, Total Fat 0.9 g, Saturated Fat 0.1 g, Cholesterol 0 mg

Sodium 76 mg, Total Carbs 26.5 g, Fiber 4 g, Sugar 20 g, Protein 1.3 g

Ingredients

- 14 ripe figs, cut in half
- ¼ cup light honey
- 1 tablespoon fresh lemon juice
- Flaky sea salt, for sprinkling

How to Prepare

1. Preheat your oven to 375°F.
2. Line a baking sheet with parchment paper.
3. Arrange the figs onto the prepared baking sheet, cut-side up.
4. Drizzle the fig halves with honey.
5. Bake for approximately 18-20 minutes or until tender and lightly caramelized.
6. Remove the baking sheet from oven and arrange the fig halves onto a platter.
7. Drizzle with lemon juice and then sprinkle with salt.
8. Serve warm.

ROASTED PEARS

Preparation time: 15 minutes

Cooking time: 25 minutes

Total time: 40 minutes

Servings: 6

Nutritional Values

Calories 222, Total Fat 10.8 g, Saturated Fat 4.4 g, Cholesterol 21 mg

Sodium 47 mg, Total Carbs 30.8 g, Fiber 3.8 g, Sugar 23.1 g, Protein 4.5 g

Ingredients

- ¼ cup pear nectar
- 3 tablespoons honey
- 2 tablespoons butter, melted
- 1 teaspoon fresh orange zest, grated
- 3 ripe medium Bosc pears, peeled and cored
- ½ cup mascarpone cheese
- 2 tablespoons powdered sugar
- 1/3 cup walnuts, chopped

How to Prepare

1. Preheat your oven to 400°F.
2. In a bowl, add the pear nectar, honey, butter, and orange zest and mix well.
3. In a large-rimmed baking sheet, arrange the pears, cut-sides down, and top with the honey mixture.
4. Roast for approximately 20–25 minutes, spooning liquid over pears occasionally.
5. Remove from the oven and transfer the pears onto serving plates with some of the cooking liquid.
6. In a bowl, add mascarpone cheese and powdered sugar and mix well.
7. Top the pears with the cheese mixture and serve with the garnishing of walnuts.

ROASTED PEACHES

Preparation time: 10 minutes

Cooking time: 30 minutes

Total time: 40 minutes

Servings: 6

Nutritional Values

Calories 145, Total Fat 9.5 g, Saturated Fat 3.6 g, Cholesterol 17 mg

Sodium 103 mg, Total Carbs 13.8 g, Fiber 1.4 g, Sugar 12.6 g, Protein 1.1 g

Ingredients

- 2 tablespoons pure maple syrup
- 2 tablespoons olive oil
- 1 tablespoon bourbon
- 1 tablespoon light brown sugar
- 1 teaspoon pure vanilla extract
- 1 teaspoon ground cinnamon
- ¼ teaspoon kosher salt
- 3 ripe peaches, halved and pitted
- 6 tablespoons whipped cream

How to Prepare

1. Preheat your oven to 350°F.
2. Lightly grease a baking sheet.
3. In a bowl, add maple syrup, olive oil, brandy, brown sugar, vanilla extract, cinnamon, and salt and beat until well blended.
4. Arrange the peach halves onto the prepared baking sheet in a single layer cut-side up.
5. Place the maple mixture over peach halves evenly.
6. Bake for approximately 30 minutes or until fork-tender.
7. Serve warm with the topping of whipped cream.

Egg Tarts

Preparation time: 20 minutes

Cooking time: 30 minutes

Total time: 50 minutes

Servings: 12

Nutritional Values

Calories 165, Total Fat 9.5 g, Saturated Fat 2.7 g, Cholesterol 51 mg

Sodium 71 mg, Total Carbs 171 g, Fiber 0.3 g, Sugar 7.9 g, Protein 3.3 g

Ingredients

- 2/3 cup hot water
- 1/3 cup plus 1 tablespoon sugar
- 1 sheet puff pastry, thawed and refrigerated
- 2 large eggs
- 1 egg yolk
- 1/3 cup evaporated milk
- ½ teaspoon vanilla extract

How to Prepare

1. Preheat your oven to 400°F.
2. Arrange a rack in the lower third position of the oven.
3. In a bowl, add hot water and sugar and stir until dissolved completely. Set aside to cool.
4. Roll out the pastry dough into 14x14-inch and then with a 4-inch cookie cutter, cut into 12 circles.
5. Arrange the pastry circles into 12 (3x1-inch) foil tart tins.
6. Arrange the foil tins onto a large baking sheet. Set aside.
7. In the bowl of sugar syrup, add the eggs, egg yolk, evaporated milk, and vanilla extract and beat until well blended.
8. Through a fine sieve, strain the egg mixture into a large bowl.
9. Carefully pour the egg mixture into tart shells, filling to just below the rim.
10. Transfer the baking sheet of tarts into the oven and bake for approximately 12–15 minutes until the edges are lightly brown.
11. Now adjust the temperature of oven to 350°F and bake for approximately 10–15 minutes further.
12. Remove the baking sheet from oven and place the tarts onto a wire rack for about 10–15 minutes before serving.

CREAM PUFFS

Preparation time: 15 minutes

Cooking time: 33 minutes

Total time: 48 minutes

Servings: 24

Nutritional Values

Calories 79, Total Fat 5.9 g, Saturated Fat 3.3 g, Cholesterol 45 mg

Sodium 60 mg, Total Carbs 5.5 g, Fiber 0.5 g, Sugar 1.4 g, Protein 1.7 g

Ingredients

- ½ cup butter
- 1 cup water
- 1 cup flour blend
- 4 large eggs
- 2/3 cup whipped cream
- 4 tablespoons powdered sugar

How to Prepare

1. Preheat your oven to 400°F.
2. Line a baking sheet with parchment paper.
3. In a pan, add butter and water and bring to a boil.
4. Boil for about 3 minutes.
5. Remove the pan of butter mixture from heat and stir in the flour until a soft dough ball forms.
6. Place the dough ball into a bowl with the eggs and with an electric mixer, mix until well blended.
7. With a small cookie scooper, place the dough balls onto the prepared baking sheet.
8. Bake for approximately 22–30 minutes or until golden lightly.
9. Remove the baking sheet of puffs from oven and transfer the puffs onto a wire rack to cool.
10. Cut each cream puff in half and fill with whipped cream.
11. Dust with powdered sugar and serve.

ALMOND BISCOTTI

Preparation time: 15 minutes

Cooking time: 15 minutes

Total time: 30 minutes

Servings: 14

Nutritional Values

Calories 94, Total Fat 6.2 g, Saturated Fat 0.4 g, Cholesterol 0 mg

Sodium 41 mg, Total Carbs 7.4 g, Fiber 1.6 g, Sugar 4.7 g, Protein 0.6 g

Ingredients

- 1¼ cups blanched almond flour
- 1 tablespoon arrowroot powder
- ¼ teaspoon baking soda
- 1/8 teaspoon salt
- ¼ cup agave nectar
- ¼ cup almonds, toasted and chopped
- 1 tablespoon fresh lemon zest, grated finely

How to Prepare

1. Preheat your oven to 350°F.
2. Line a cookie sheet with parchment paper.
3. In a bowl, mix together flour, arrowroot powder, baking soda, and salt.
4. Add agave nectar and mix until a dough forms.
5. Fold in almonds and lemon zest.
6. Cut the dough into 2 equal-sized portions.
7. Shape each dough portion in loaves.
8. Arrange the loaves onto the prepared cookie sheet about 4 inches apart.
9. Bake for approximately 15 minutes.
10. Remove the cookie sheet from oven and set aside to cool for about 1 hour.
11. With a knife, cut the loaves into 1-inch slices diagonally.
12. Now, set the temperature of oven to 300°F.
13. Bake for approximately 12–15 minutes more.
14. Remove the cookie sheet from oven and place onto a wire rack to cool for about 5 minutes.
15. Now, invert the biscotti onto the wire rack to cool before serving.

BLUEBERRY CAKE

Preparation time: 10 minutes

Cooking time: 15 minutes

Total time: 25 minutes

Servings: 15

Nutritional Values

Calories 171, Total Fat 5.1 g, Saturated Fat 2.8 g, Cholesterol 36 mg

Sodium 373 mg, Total Carbs 26.5 g, Fiber 1.2 g, Sugar 5.6 g, Protein 4.9 g

Ingredients

- 3 cups all-purpose flour
- 2 tablespoons sugar
- 2 tablespoons baking powder
- 2 teaspoons salt
- 2 large eggs
- 2½ cups skim milk
- 1/3 cup butter, melted
- 2 cups fresh blueberries

How to Prepare

1. Preheat your oven to 425°F.
2. Line an 18x13-inch sheet pan with a greased parchment paper.
3. In a bowl, add flour, sugar, baking powder, and salt and mix well.
4. Add the eggs, milk, and butter and mix until smooth.
5. Place half of the mixture onto the prepared sheet pan and with a spatula, spread in an even layer.
6. Sprinkle the blueberries on top evenly.
7. Now, spread the remaining flour mixture over the blueberries evenly.
8. Bake for approximately 15 minutes or until a toothpick inserted in the center comes out clean.
9. Remove the sheet pan of cake from the oven and place onto a wire rack to cool for about 10-15 minutes.
10. Then turn the cake onto the wire rack to cool completely before serving.
11. Cut the cake into desired-sized pieces and serve.

Pumpkin Cake

Preparation time: 10 minutes

Cooking time: 23 minutes

Total time: 33 minutes

Servings: 16

Nutritional Values

Calories 185, Total Fat 7.2 g, Saturated Fat 0.7 g, Cholesterol 1 mg

Sodium 157 mg, Total Carbs 28.5 g, Fiber 1.3 g, Sugar 14.5 g, Protein 2.2 g

Ingredients

- 2 cups all-purpose flour, sifted
- 1 tablespoon baking powder
- ½ teaspoon baking soda
- 2 teaspoons pumpkin pie spice
- 1 teaspoon ground cinnamon
- ¾ teaspoon salt
- 1 (15-ounce) can pumpkin puree
- 1½ cups brown sugar
- ½ cup milk
- ½ cup canola oil
- 2 teaspoons vanilla extract

How to Prepare

1. Preheat your oven to 350°F.
2. Line a 9x13-inch sheet pan with greased parchment paper.
3. In a bowl, add flour, baking powder, baking soda, spices, and salt and mix well.
4. In a separate bowl, add remaining ingredients (except for powdered sugar) and beat until well blended.
5. In the bowl of pumpkin mixture, add the flour mixture and mix until just blended.
6. Place the mixture into the prepared sheet pan and with a spatula, spread in an even layer.
7. Place the sheet pan of cake in the oven and bake for approximately 25–30 minutes or until a wooden toothpick inserted in the center of cake comes out clean.
8. Remove the sheet pan of cake from the oven and place onto a wire rack to cool for about 10–12 minutes.
9. Then turn the cake onto the wire rack to cool completely before serving.
10. Cut the cake into desired-sized pieces and serve.

KEY LIME PIE

Preparation time: 15 minutes

Cooking time: 25 minutes

Total time: 40 minutes

Servings: 15

Nutritional Values

Calories 363, Total Fat 18.7 g, Saturated Fat 9.9 g, Cholesterol 129 mg

Sodium 215 mg, Total Carbs 44.8 g, Fiber 0 g, Sugar 31.3 g, Protein 6.7 g

Ingredients

Crust

- 1 (14.1-ounce) box refrigerated pie crusts, softened

Filling

- 2 (14-ounce) cans sweetened condensed milk
- ¾ cup fresh key lime juice
- 6 egg yolks

Topping

- 2 cups heavy whipping cream
- 3 tablespoons sugar
- 1 tablespoon lime peel, grated

How to Prepare

1. Preheat your oven to 450°F.
2. Place the pie crusts onto a lightly floured surface and unroll them.
3. Place 1 crust over another crust and roll into a 17x12-inch rectangle.
4. Arrange the rolled crust into a 15x10x1-inch sheet pan, pressing firmly into corners and sides.
5. With a fork, poke the crust evenly.
6. Bake for approximately 9–11 minutes or until golden brown.
7. Remove the sheet pan from oven and place onto a wire rack for about 15 minutes.
8. Now adjust the temperature of oven to 350°F.
9. **For filling:** In a medium bowl, add condensed milk, lime juice, and egg yolks and beat until well blended.
10. Place the filling mixture over the cooled crust and spread evenly.

11. Bake for approximately 10–12 minutes or until filling is set.
12. Remove the sheet pan of pie from oven and place onto a wire rack for about 15 minutes.
13. With a plastic wrap, cover the pie and refrigerate for at least 1½ hours.
14. **For topping:** In a bowl, add whipping cream and with an electric mixer, beat on high speed until thickened.
15. Add the sugar and with an electric mixer, beat until soft peaks form.
16. Spread cream mixture over the chilled pie and top with lime peel.
17. Cut into desired-sized pieces and serve.

CHOCOLATE CAKE

Preparation time: 15 minutes

Cooking time: 35 minutes

Total time: 50 minutes

Servings: 15

Nutritional Values

Calories 575, Total Fat 20.6 g, Saturated Fat 10 g, Cholesterol 81mg

Sodium 346 mg, Total Carbs 97.1 g, Fiber 2.8 g, Sugar 76.2 g, Protein 5.8 g

Ingredients

<u>Cake</u>
- 2 cups all-purpose flour
- 2/3 cup unsweetened cocoa powder
- 1 teaspoon baking soda
- ¼ teaspoon baking powder
- 1 teaspoon ground cinnamon
- ¼ teaspoon table salt
- 1 2/3 cups light brown sugar
- 3 large eggs
- 2 teaspoons vanilla extract
- 1 cup mayonnaise
- 1 1/3 cups hot water

<u>Frosting</u>
- 1 (8-ounce) package cream cheese, softened
- ½ cup butter, softened
- 2 teaspoons vanilla extract
- 1 (32-ounce) package powdered sugar
- ½ cup unsweetened cocoa powder
- 5–6 tablespoons heavy cream

How to Prepare

1. Preheat your oven to 350°F.
2. Lightly grease a 9x13-inch sheet pan with cooking spray.
3. **For cake:** In a bowl, add flour, cocoa powder, baking soda, baking powder, cinnamon, and salt and mix well.
4. In a separate bowl, add the brown sugar, eggs, and vanilla extract and with an electric mixer, beat on medium-high speed until light.
5. Add the mayonnaise and then beat on low speed until combined.
6. Add the flour mixture, alternately with hot water, and beat on low speed until just combined.
7. Place the mixture into the prepared sheet pan and with a spatula, spread in an even layer.
8. Bake for approximately 31–35 minutes or until a wooden toothpick inserted in the center comes out clean.
9. Remove the sheet pan of cake from the oven and place onto a wire rack to cool for about 10–12 minutes.
10. Then turn the cake onto the wire rack to cool completely before frosting.
11. **For frosting:** In a bowl, add the cream cheese, butter, and vanilla extract and beat with an electric mixer until creamy.
12. In a separate bowl, add the powdered sugar and cocoa and mix well.
13. Slowly, add the sugar mixture into the butter mixture alternately with cream and beat on low speed until well blended.
14. Now, beat on medium speed until light and fluffy.
15. Spread the frosting over the cake evenly.
16. Cut the cake into desired-sized pieces and serve.

CONCLUSION

Whether you are roasting vegetables, meat, seafood, or baking cookies or cakes, sheet pans offer a large cooking surface area to provide heat to every bit of food evenly. Sheet pans can be used to cook a variety of meals using different seasonings and flavors. Now you can cook all sorts of meals using sheet pans at home as we brought you the best of sheet pan recipes in this cookbook. There are recipes for breakfast, making snacks, lunch, dinner, desserts, etc. All you need to do is get the right sheet pan for the right time and let's get started!

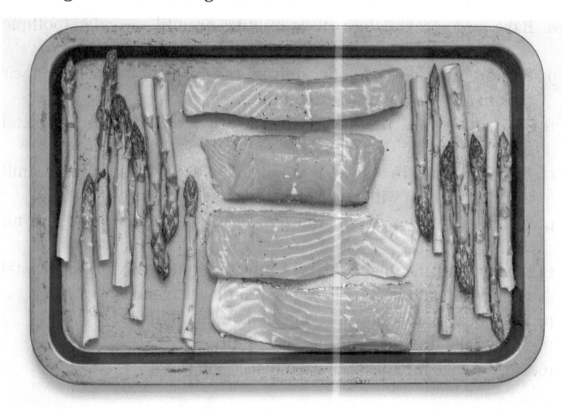

Made in United States
Troutdale, OR
12/05/2023